Empowering Change

The role of people management

Christopher Ridgeway
and
Brian Wallace

INSTITUTE OF PERSONNEL
AND DEVELOPMENT

First published in 1994
Reprinted 1997

Typeset by Photoprint, Torquay
and printed in Great Britain by
Short Run Press, Exeter

British Library Cataloguing in Publication Data

*A catalogue record for this book is available from the
British Library*

ISBN 0–85292–548–4

**INSTITUTE OF PERSONNEL
AND DEVELOPMENT**
IPD House, Camp Road, London SW19 4UX
Tel: 0181 971 9000   Fax: 0181 263 3333
Registered office as above. Registered Charity No. 1038333
A company limited by guarantee. Registered in England No. 2931892

Empowering Change

Brian Wallace and **Dr Christopher Ridgeway** are partners in the ODL Consultancy Partnership in Eton, formed 20 years ago, which specialises in counselling senior management teams on business-related strategies for change, the creation and assessment of competencies needed for future leaders, and overall management development strategies. ODL's clients include leading multinationals and 'blue chip' companies such as Shell International, the Allied Lyons Group, Reckitt and Colman, J P Morgan & Co, Sedgwick International, Unilever, British Sugar, Abbey National, BT and British Gas. They are the authors of *Leadership for Strategic Change*, published by the IPD in 1996.

Brian Wallace moved from internal into external consultancy. He worked for British Aerospace, ICI and finally Shell Chemicals, as head of organisation and management development, before forming ODL. Over the last 20 years he has been involved in board-level consultancy advising on the formulation of strategies for change, and counselling MDs and director teams on the right philosophy and the role of leadership in such initiatives. He has spoken at business schools in the UK and USA on change leadership and across the IPD network on HR's role and influence.

Dr Christopher Ridgeway is a chartered occupational and counselling psychologist. Before moving into consultancy some 15 years ago he held senior international HR management positions with the Burton Group and Champion Inc. His distinctive business orientation is most unusual in a psychologist and he can offer consultancy clients both ever-increasing insights into the dynamics of the individual and analysis of the factors that maximise business performance. He was a founding director of the Harley Group, a regional director with Hay Management Consultants and MD of Psyconsult, a subsidiary of Manpower. He is an active researcher and a contributor of many challenging articles to British and European psychological and management journals.

Contents

Introduction   vii

1. Empowering Change – An Introduction   1
2. A History of Change   11
3. Leadership Values in Change   22
4. The HR Function in Transition   35
5. Managing Restructuring – A Case Study   50
6. Internationalising Business – A Case Study   76
7. Achieving Market Leadership – A Case Study   98
8. Integrating Mergers and Acquisitions – A
   Case Study   110
9. Thriving on Change and Supporting the Casualties   129
10. Managing the new Manager   142
11. Rebuilding Trust   150
12. Judging the Individual's Capacity to Change   163
13. The Future – Developing Change Leadership
    Potential   181
14. The Future – The HR Professional as a Strategic
    Partner   193

Empowering Change – A Postscript   202
About the Contributors   207
Index   208

To our wives Eleanor and Tina,
for their continuous support and encouragement

◼ Introduction

Our aim in writing this book has been to focus on practical, business-related actions which will deliver successful change. However, change in complex organisations, faced with a rapidly changing business environment, is not a simple and straightforward process. We have set out, therefore, to define a set of principles and concepts important to the planning and implementation of change together with a series of case studies which describe the courses of action followed by actual managers. In this way, we hope to achieve the right balance between theory and practice. Our 'theory' is not derived from academic premises but from extensive research on and experience of the effective responses to change by managers in real-life organisations, which results in an empirical and practical rather than a theoretical approach. Our measure of success would be if both line managers and the HR professional discover practical strategies for their particular change problems.

A broad perspective

In this context, we have chosen to include as broad a range of perspectives as possible. To do this, we include insights on the change process from:

- the Line Directors whom we have counselled through major change assignments
- the HR Directors and Management Development Managers, who examine their role and influence with the Line
- the occupational psychologists employed to assess, develop and counsel individual managers through change
- the organisational development specialists advising on the whole cultural change process.

This broad, multi-faceted, perspective demonstrates our belief that change needs to be viewed from standpoints of the business, the line manager, the HR professional and the individuals and teams involved.

Our team of contributors are:

Rien Waale, Chemical Coordinator, Shell International, whose philosophy of corporate restructuring is illustrated in Chapter 5

Leonard Sheen, HR Director Europe and Far East, Hiram Walker Group (an Allied-Lyons subsidiary), who presents a fascinating case history of business start up in Eastern Europe in Chapter 6

John Refaussé, Director of HR Development, Hiram Walker, whose work on 'Developing the International Manager' for the whole Allied-Lyons Group is also described in Chapter 6

Trevor Johnson, HR Director, Reckitt & Colman Products Ltd, whose work on 'Achieving Market Leadership' in both the pharmaceutical and household products businesses is described in Chapter 7

David Patterson, Corporate Affairs, General Manager, Zurich Insurance, whose experience in successfully integrating the old Municipal Mutual Insurance into a major European insurer is described in Chapter 8

Ashley Wood, Manager, Personnel Development, Meyer International, who together with one of our psychologists, Paul Henry, describes their experiences on the impact of leaner, flatter organisations on the career expectations of younger managers in Chapter 10

Paul Henry, Senior Consultant, ODL, who moved from a career in engineering to occupational psychology. His interest is in the dynamic learning organisation of the future

Dr Lea Brindle, a Chartered Occupational Psychologist who is Principal of Psychological Solutions Consultancy and also works closely with ODL, describes his research on assessing and counselling redundant managers in Chapter 9. He identifies the key characteristics of employees who thrive on change and suggests ways to support, train and develop the inevitable casualties. In Chapter 13, he presents the ODL research on how to assess and develop change leadership potential, ie the ability of some managers to go beyond coping with change and to find proactive means of initiating it.

The prime contributors are the MDs, Directors, Managers and Staff of over 200 companies around the world with whom we have worked on major change strategies over the last 20 years. The lessons drawn are ours, but it was their response to change which provided the real learning.

People make the difference

This mixture of drawing lessons from real experience, the insights of the Line Director and HR Professional, the psychological impact on the individual, the overall organisational change process, we believe provides a rich menu. Coupled with our research work, it should enable businesses to plan for the future in an increasingly complex and rapidly changing world.

This book is about people making the difference in change. The title and the core messages running through it reflect our firm conviction that if people, at whatever level, are excited and challenged to work together and achieve beneficial change, then this will truly make the difference.

1

Empowering Change – An Introduction

Why call a book *Empowering Change*? As one of our more hard nosed colleagues would say: 'Isn't this just another set of buzz words – a flavour of the month catchphrase?'

Our response, which we believe is not a defence, is that change is about people: people as individuals, as team members, as company personnel – all striving to adapt and respond to the rapidly changing business environment, all working to gain a competitive advantage. If people do not feel motivated and empowered by change, how is the release of energy essential to innovation and creative development going to emerge? It is people who are adaptive, responsive and creative not organisations and systems. If we cannot realise that potential in and through change, then how can we create the kind of organisations needed for future success? A factor which is critical to successful change planning is that it should be empowering. Hence our title, which reflects our beliefs and values and which our experience of advising on successful change management over a period of 40 years reinforces.

This book has been written in order to pose fundamental questions to managers and to their Human Resource advisers concerning their basic beliefs and values in both considering and planning change. Our experience suggests that without empowerment, change can become mechanistic, a top-down imposition from which no fundamental change actually results. In most cases, a style of leadership behaviour which lacks values will invariably result in a mistrust of change on the part of personnel. The ensuing resistance to change which will result can be characterised by suspicion of management's motives, internal politics, rumours proliferating, energy consumed in speculation, and high levels of ambiguity and uncertainty which can become the seedcorn around which an inward

Figure 1.1
A cycle of frustration

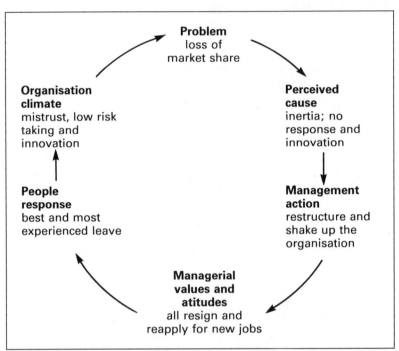

looking, unhealthy culture can grow. Change can become a battle ground on which there are no real winners, producing a lose/lose situation for all involved.

What we have found is that valueless change, which does not seek to empower, can result in a cycle of frustration (see Figure 1.1). Whereas, a response which *does* value people could be illustrated as in Figure 1.2.

A change partnership

Our notion of empowering change is addressed to line managers who are responsible for change leadership and to

Figure 1.2
Empowering change

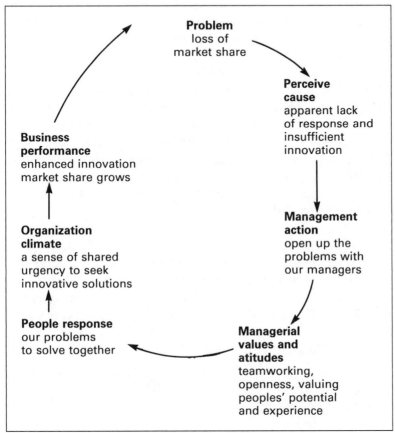

their Human Resource advisers who act as counsellors on change. The proposition which we develop throughout is that effective and sustaining change requires a change partnership between the line and the Human Resource functions.

It will become apparent that we throw down many gauntlets both to line managers and Human Resource specialists. We do so because we know from our experience that self-questioning and challenge lie at the core of the process of empowering managers to empower their organisations. Change is not about certainty and predictability. We would suggest that managers need to learn about themselves and their own values before they have the right to lead others through a change process. Successful change requires that the leaders of change adapt their own behaviour to fit the new style of operation required. If they are successful, they will become the role models for the future. Much unsuccessful change results from leaders of organisations demanding change from others rather than themselves. Our book seeks to illustrate that successful change is not a one-off exercise, but a permanent, on-going and tough challenge to all involved. Learning and adaptation may not be easy, but they can be fun and stimulating. Personal growth, innovation, and striving for competitive advantage are all strong indicators of a healthy and successful business.

We seek to address, also, the beliefs and values of HR professionals. The proposition which we develop is that, to be successful in change, the HR function needs to be a challenging strategic partner with the line management, not only on the mechanics of the change process but also on the fundamentals of change. The role and influence of HR professionals as the custodians of 'people values' are central to the theme developed throughout our book.

A language of change

In the early chapters of the book, we establish a basic language of change and offer a range of ideas on formulating effective change strategies. Fundamental issues which we address include:

Change planning
- How can we ensure that we capture the hearts and minds of our people?
- Should change be an evolutionary or revolutionary process?
- Should we impose change or consult our people? Do we have the time?

- What are the vital steps which we need to follow to ensure successful change?
- Who are the critical stakeholders in change? How do we plan to involve them?

Change leading
- As the directors responsible, what leadership approach should we follow?
- How can we ensure that we don't take our sights off the business issues?
- How can we ensure that we gain a competitive advantage through change?
- Our responsibility is to take the tough decisions; people know that change is the name of the game, so why should we worry about change planning?

Change counselling
- What role and influence should the HR function perform and exert?
- Managers are paid to manage; isn't our role just change facilitation?
- How do we ensure that the right balance of effort is preserved between the *leavers* and the *stayers*?
- What battles are we likely to have to fight, if we believe in empowering change?

Our choice of case material in the middle chapters aims to illustrate how various change managers have effectively resolved these and other issues.

The change agenda

As well as posing questions, our book seeks to indicate a number of practical solutions to the extending range of change issues with which management is faced. Our illustrations are drawn from practical case material and they seek to show how the managements concerned faced up to the change challenge. Their value is, therefore, that they underline the significance of our basic premise that successful change management requires a continuous process of planning, acting, reviewing, learning and adapting.

The chapters which contain case histories cover a change agenda consisting of:

- managing structural change
- achieving market leadership
- internationalising management
- managing mergers and acquisitions
- business start up in Eastern Europe

The casualties of change

The recent past has been one of the worst and most pervasive recessions faced by businesses in the UK. It has under-standably resulted in many casualties of change. The large numbers of managers and staff who have experienced enforced or voluntary redundancies represent a visible challenge to the consciences and values of their previous employers. At the same time, one significant growth area, sadly, has been in career counselling and redeployment advice. Those who offer such services require their 'clients' to honestly reappraise themselves and their career track records in the context of in-depth explorations of career successes and failures, personal ambitions and motivations, personal atti-tudes and problems, distinctive and marketable competences and experience.

We believe that our work – in counselling over 3,000 managers together with the ensuing analysis and research – can provides useful insights into the problems of redundancy and redeployment, many of which have direct relevance to the questions addressed in subsequent chapters, such as:

- What types of people are most liable to be made redundant?
- What are the implications for HR planning?
- How can permanent casualties be avoided?
- How can stress problems be anticipated?
- Who are the most successful in finding redeployment?
- Who are the people who struggle most?
- What counselling and support is needed both to repair individuals' confidence and energise them to achieve redeployment?
- What are the general lessons drawn about the casualties of change?

Critical success factors in change management

In the several discussions which address aspects of successful change management, we draw together various strands of thinking which stem from:

- our general consultancy experience
- hypotheses and theories which we have applied and tested over time
- an interrogation of the lessons drawn from a broad array of change case histories, some of which are included, here.

We seek to establish which factors are essential to effective and sustaining change management. Topics addressed include:

- appropriate leadership styles and philosophies
- the types of change and the different approaches suited to them
- the role and influence of the HR function
- critical phases in the processes of change planning and management
- the actions needed to build the readiness and receptiveness to change
- the need for a change agent/support resource

- balancing the effort needed to support both the casualties of change and those who have to make the transformed organisation work
- processes for reviewing the effectiveness of change
- the integration of change into the normal, on-going processes of management.

Checklists of important principles, strategies and questions for managers and HR professionals faced with change are provided at the end of several chapters.

The future – the manager as a leader of change

Throughout our book, emphasis is focused upon the central importance of the change values and behaviour of managers as the leaders of change. We present the fundamental proposition that the leadership of change is a core competence of the successful director and manager of the future. We develop the proposition's implications for:

- recruiting managers and staff who have appropriate qualities and abilities
- assessing managers as potential change leaders
- developing managers as effective change leaders
- career mapping as a process for broadening managers' change repertoire.

We have carried out extensive research on the characteristics of 'the effective change manager', and present here an examination of the distinctive personal motivations and competences required to achieve effectiveness and success in this challenging capacity.

We believe that this work provides fresh insights for use in

- management development
- manpower assessment and planning

Future business success, in a rapidly changing and increasingly complex and competitive business environment, will require

- change leadership competences which distinguish one business from its competitors
- management processes which scan the environment, both externally and internally, and anticipate the need for change
- management processes and practices which engender a climate for continuous adaptation and improvement
- the creation of an organisational culture which empowers individuals and encourages personal risk taking, assertiveness and innovation.

We indicate the processes required to develop the high performing, change-skilled, organisation of the future.

The future – the HR function as a strategic partner in change

In sponsoring this book, the Institute of Personnel and Development intended to provide both challenges and practical advice to HR professionals. At the end of each chapter, we raise questions about effective change management, or draw out important lessons from the preceding discussion, which we hope will serve to stimulate critical reflection and debate.

The final chapter introduces a number of frameworks for the future roles, objectives and requisite competences of the HR specialist as 'change agent'. The models presented are built around the notions of the HR function as

- *a custodian of personnel practices*
- *the developer of people*
- *a strategic change partner*

It is our experience that in advising on change management

the HR function faces a number of difficult problems. For
example:

- Line Managers have the responsibility and authority to
  reshape their businesses and organisations. What right do
  HR professionals have to challenge them?
- Isn't the role of HR specifically and only to facilitate change
  by ensuring that policies and procedures are in place to
  enable management to act as it sees fit?
- Change imposes a considerable demand on the HR function
  in respect of staff communication, redundancy counselling,
  staff selection, redefining organisations and jobs, and evaluating new jobs. If HR professionals do all of these things,
  aren't they already fulfilling their responsibilities? Should
  they seek to increase their sphere of influence further?

We pose a series of questions on the values involved in and
required by empowering change. The principal challenge is to
the courage and convictions of HR professionals. Our belief is
that the HR function should aim to be more than just a change
facilitator: our proposal is that the creation of healthy and
innovative organisations for the future will be best achieved
through a creative partnership between HR and line management functions. If our book influences HR and line managers
to develop such partnerships, in seeking empowerment
through change, it will have made a useful contribution to
current personnel management thinking.

2

▚ A History of Change

The last 20 years has seen a significant evolution in thinking about change management, making it obvious that the socio-economic climate of the day is a clear determinant of the focus for, and attitudes to, change. Nowadays, change is endemic. Business leaders realise that change is constantly on their agenda: managers and staff anticipate and fear it, and the shareholders and the City expect it. A new breed of management is emerging, a 'tribe of company doctors' who are appointed to turn businesses around, and to take tough decisions with no sympathy for the past. People and their experience are often seen as dispensable commodities. This new-broom thinking is a prevalent currency. The rewards are high for success, though failure is a very public price to pay.

Does this scenario however negate our philosophy of empowering values? Many would argue that success breeds success. Clearly, for the winners, it is empowering; but what of the losers and the underlying climate of fear created? The current attitude to change illustrates markedly the dilemmas in change planning: whatever approach is followed, there is inevitably a profit and loss statement. The requisite skill is to ensure that the consequences of a particular approach to change are anticipated, and then managed in a way which facilitates the empowerment sought.

The lessons of the history of change are worth considering. Table 2.1 is drawn from our experience over the last 20 years and illustrates the process of evolution in terms of both the business focus/rationale for change and the attitudes to change management which have prevailed.

Table 2.1
The evolution of change thinking

Period	Focus	Objective	Change ingredients
1960s	Systems engineering	To enhance efficiency through the definition and standardisation of works practices, and the tight measurement of performance coupled with incentified bonus schemes	• work study • job measurement • efficiency/productivity measurement • job/work redesign • job performance bonuses
ODL illustration: Plessey introducing job redesign into the wiring line where the teams were asked to organise their work patterns and inspection procedures			
1970s	Culture change	To introduce flexible working and so realise the potential in people	• job/work design • teamworking • job enrichment/motivation • leadership training/ managerial GRID • interpersonal sensitivity training/T groups
ODL illustration: ICI investing in a major training programme across all management levels, aimed at questioning leadership approach and attitudes to people, and encouraging team and cross-team working and improvement planning			

Period	Focus	Objective	Change ingredients
late 1970s	Organisation redesign	To structure a flexible response to the changing business environment	• matrix management systems • centralisation vs devolution • strategic planning and review
ODL illustration: Shell International devolving responsibility to the country operations and realigning the corporate Headquarter's roles			
late 1970s onwards	Introduction of psychometrics	To ensure that the right people are selected, developed and promoted	• psychometric testing • aptitude testing • selection panels • selection centres • assessment centres
ODL Illustration: Cable & Wireless carrying out managerial strength audits of all their management levels			

Table 2.1
continued

Period	Focus	Objective	Change ingredients
1980s	Performance management	To motivate and reward people for measurable performance	• management by objectives • staff appraisal • reward systems • career management
ODL Illustration: Lloyds Bank introducing job accountability definition and training in appraisal skills			
1980s	Business internationalisation	To develop business on a world market scale	• IT systems • telecommunications • planning conferences • strategic business units • portfolio management • the international manager • cross-cultural awareness • mission and values
ODL Illustration: Hiram Walker's start up of an apple juice factory in Eastern Europe			

Period	Focus	Objective	Change ingredients
1980s	Customer focus	To establish a customer/market orientation to business growth	• 'just in time' schemes • total quality management • market led planning • service/performance standards • customer care campaigns
ODL Illustration: Grant Thornton training programmes for all management and partner levels on client management skills			
mid 1980s	Management competences	To select and develop the people who will be high performers in the future business environment	• competency profiling • 'Best' vs 'the rest' comparisons • behavioural event interviewing • development/assessment centres • individual development planning • manager as a 'coach'
ODL Illustration: Manchester Airport exercise, establishing the managerial competences needed from the top to the bottom of the organisation to establish the transition from local authority control to international airport			

Table 2.1
continued

Period	Focus	Objective	Change ingredients
late 1980s	The flatter organisation	To shorten the lines of communication and the speed and quality of decision making	• broadened spans of controls • management by objectives/exception • devolution of responsibilities and authorities • organisation re-design • reduction of overheads/bureaucracy
ODL Illustration: British Sugar Research Laboratories reducing management levels and defining the competencies, both scientific and managerial, needed to move from level to level			
early 1990s	Process re-engineering	To focus on the critical management processes which deliver competitive advantages	• critical success factor analysis • task forces on process improvements • team/cross-team working • continuous improvement thinking

Lessons from a history of change

Growing managerial sophistication

This 'history of change' is illustrative of the evolving understanding of the importance which management now places on
the understanding of the human dynamics of organisations.
The clear belief emerges that 'if we get our own house in order
and focus the thinking of our organisation's people then this
will deliver a competitive advantage'. Over the period described,
the most dramatic shift is away from a simplistic view of
organisations in terms of structures and systems, towards a
more sophisticated approach which embraces a greater understanding of people, their motivations, attitudes and competences, as well as the importance of organisational culture
for performance.

'Hard'/'soft' management attitudes

Another significant feature is the apparent fluctuation between
the 'hard' and 'soft' approaches to change management. The
'hard' approach would encompass a business focus on strategy,
structures, systems, productivity, performance, organisational
efficiency and customer service. The 'soft' approach would
focus rather on the 'people' aspects of organisations, which
would enbrace culture, leadership style and behaviour, individual competences, aptitudes and motivation, and internal
management processes. All these factors are vital to effective
change management. The problem for management is how to
achieve the right balance.

Our history of change management appears to indicate an
emerging cyclical pattern of an era of a 'hard' focus followed by
an era emphasising 'soft' factors, and vice versa. (see Table
2.2).

The notion of compensating eras of change management
reinforces the need to see change as a continuous rather than

Table 2.2

The 'hard'/'soft' approach to change management

Hard factors	Soft factors
Systems engineering – efficiency, productivity, performance incentives	*Culture change* – leadership, motivation, sensitivity
Organisation redesign – structure, accountabilities, authorities	*Psychological measurement* – psychometrics, aptitudes, selection
Performance management – objectives, appraisal, reward	*Business internationalisation* – communication/planning process, cultural awareness
Customer focus – customer service, TQM, market orientation	*Managerial competences* – profiling, motives and competences, selection processes
Flatter organisation – overheads, bureaucracy, communications, decision making	*Process re-engineering* – critical success factors, key processes, temporary organisation systems, cultural change

interruptive process. For both the leaders of change and the HR function as 'change consultants', this becomes a critical part of formulating strategies for change. Effective change management is about maintaining and sustaining the balance. A 'hard nosed' bottom-line focus needs to encompass an awareness of the impact on the people system, which will eventually require effort at repairing and rebuilding staff confidence and commitment. The message is that empowering people will always matter, if change is to have a positive impact on organisational behaviour and performance.

This balancing approach is well illustrated by the model

Table 2.3
A 'hard'/'soft' model for managing diversity

Corporate	
Corporate/Hard	Corporate/Soft
<ul><li>business objectives/ strategies</li><li>structure</li><li>systems</li><li>planning</li><li>management</li></ul>	<ul><li>superordinate goals</li><li>culture/shared values</li><li>company style</li><li>behaviour norms</li><li>status elements</li></ul>
Technical Economic	Social
'Hard'	'Soft'
Individual/Hard	Individual/Soft
<ul><li>staff reward system</li><li>job design</li><li>job clarification</li><li>rules and regulations</li><li>legislative measures</li></ul>	<ul><li>knowledge and skills</li><li>attitudes</li><li>values</li><li>personal style</li><li>career aspirations/ expectations</li></ul>
Individual	

developed in Aat Brakel's book of Shell case histories, *People and Organizations Interacting*. In the concluding chapter, entitled 'Managing Diversity' he draws his lessons from a 'hard'/'soft' model (see Table 2.3).

Brakel's analysis of lessons on managing diversity highlights the need to consider 'the connections' involved. From our experience, the successful planning and management of change demands a recognition of the essential interdependencies of the 'hard' and 'soft' factors.

For example, with reference to Table 2.3, if management embarks on a programme of major restructuring, the requisite effort will be in:

(a) the *individual/hard* sector, to consider the impact of

change on individual roles and rewards, and as such to
institutionalise change within the on-going management
procedures and systems

(b) the *corporate-soft* sector, to inspire staff on the future
mission and values of the organisation – a shift which
repairs and rebuilds relationships around the proposition
of a shared, challenging and motivating vision and a
restatement of managerial values and expectations

and

(c) the *individual/soft* sector, which reviews the competences
needed for high performance within the restructured
organisation which again emphasises an interest in staff
concerns about future career options and the specific
implications for individual growth.

There is a clear need in change planning to consider the values
and approaches requried to re-empower people. Brakel's
conclusions also highlight the challenge faced by the leaders of
change in managing both the diversity and the problems
involved. Our proposition is that the Director/Senior Manager
of the future needs to have the competences, motivation and
experience to deal with the complexities of strategic change
management. Chapter 12 deals with the demands and competences needed for the successful leader of change.

Successful change

This discussion indicates that successful change must encompass a broad range of considerations. The critical success
factors include:

- the need for a discernible and measurable business focus
- the impact of leadership philosophy and approach in managing change, which, for the staff involved, will become the
  perceived management philosophy in practice

- a strong external focus which considers both customer and competitive positioning
- an emphasis on organisation simplification and, hence, the capacity to respond to market changes quickly and in line with overall strategy and policy
- the capacity for recognising and ensuring that the requirement for individual, team and organisational empowerment is considered
- the need to institute change with the established goal-setting, appraisal and reward processes
- the recognition that change is an on-going process, not a punctuated, interruptive, tactical response
- the awareness that change is a phased evolution: the focus of one phase will need compensation in the next phase
- the acknowledgement that culture change is an essential underpinning to the strategic change thrust, without which the construct may be different but the behaviour and norms unchanged.

3

Leadership Values in Change

Empowering values

In earlier chapters, we have emphasised the importance of clear leadership values in change planning. Our 'history of change' depicted the fluctuation in management thinking from 'hard' to 'soft' attitudes. The message here is that the business change need is imperative; yet to neglect the people and cultural implications could well put at risk the positive behaviours, responses and attitudes sought. This is especially pertinent if the underpinning assumption is that successful business organisations of the future will need to be able to adapt and respond to the changing business environment in a natural as distinct from change-enforced manner. A positive management attitude, which considers empowerment a part of change planning, will not only facilitate the successful implementation of a specific change initiative, but also lay the foundations for creating an adaptive and responsive organisational culture.

Table 3.1 illustrates the shift required from a 'devaluing' to an 'empowering' set of *leadership values in change*.

For the HR function this required shift issues a prime challenge, if those concerned wish to be effective and influential internal change consultants and facilitators. Too often the business argument for change can cause these 'values in change' to become submerged and judged as unimportant. The role of HR must be to ensure that they are kept on the surface. The risk is that the managers and staff impacted by change will be exploring the real intentions, underlying motives, and leadership behaviour in change for clues about the future implications for themselves. To feel themselves victims of change can clearly sensitise people. It raises questions and can sow the seeds for the growth of negative attitudes and responses to change.

Table 3.1

Leadership values in change

Devaluing Away from:	Empowering Towards:
change is the sole responsibility of Senior Management	change and continuous improvement are challenges for, and the responsibility of, all levels in the organisation
change is about the business need	change and adaptation are vital to the growth and survival of all individuals, teams and organisations
change focuses on strategy, organisational structure and systems	change in complex organisational systems is about people and their responses to the market place
change is driven by the market-place and customer need	change is about empowering the management of the customer interfaces to deliver quality service
change is an evil which faces us in hard times	change is continuous and an on-going process
change management interrupts our running of the business	change management, learning and adaptation are central to future business success
the role of management is to both diagnose the need and direct change strategies	the building of a responsive and adaptive culture is a key leadership responsibility
successful change is about overcoming people's blocks and resistance to change	people are driven by overcoming difficulty and grow in confidence to face new challenges
the successful manager delivers results	the high performance manager of the future sees his role in scanning the need for, shaping and leading the process of change
management's role is in defining change plans and communicating them	people involvement in change planning will result in greater ownership and commitment
change thinking needs to be confidential	openness on change issues values people and stimulates a positive response
people have to understand that change is inevitable	people recognise that adaptation is vital to personal growth
resistance and inertia to change inhibits our performance	people are innovative and knowledgeable and can help us resolve change issues
people should not be involved in change considerations	people will participate constructively
mistrusting people	trusting people

Future change initiatives will be likely to trigger these undercurrents and so heighten the resistance to change.

The business need and people responses

Value-based thinking requires management to believe that empowering people through change will make the difference. A major block here could be that Senior Management would argue that top-down driven change is needed, because the business organisation has not adapted to market change, that it is inertia and resistance to change which inhibit responsiveness. Why, then, try to empower people who demonstrably are not committed to change?

The resolution of this dilemma is central to the change argument. Too often Senior Management can persuade themselves that it is people, and not themselves, who create the blocks to change. This may be further reinforced by the proposition that firm top-down leadership is needed when the going gets tough.

An argument often raised in our consultancy experience is that radical, tough change is necessary to shock people into action. This is often reinforced by an attitude which says: 'If you cannot stand the heat in the kitchen, then you are free to leave.' The risk is that, in recession, people may feel forced to conform. Economic times can, however, change and the best people, who have hidden their feelings, may decide to move on to more valuing companies.

What, then, could be a way forward which avoids these potential 'win/lose' extremes?

A new philosophy of management

Managerial values are determined substantially by:

- an individual's own experience of being managed through change, in which bosses' behaviour can become either a role model or an anti-role model. The lessons are drawn from one's own feelings and reactions
- the assumptions that people make about management and organisational life. If one believes that management is about authority, status, direction and control, and that people are a means to an end, then a conclusion about being directive can readily be drawn. Whereas, if the belief is that management is to do with leadership and achieving the difference – the competitive edge, through people – then an empowering attitude will exist.

A key task for the HR function is to ensure, through management education and development, that change-orientated values are thoroughly considered. To wait for the next major change drive could limit the amount of time available for reflection and questioning.

Table 3.2 illustrates the move towards a new philosophy of management, based on certain underpinning management beliefs and attitudes. It describes the transition away from 'static' concepts of organisational life towards a 'dynamic and adaptive' view. This serves to further illustrate the notion of 'empowering change' in practice.

In a management training environment, the consequences of these different philosophies can be fully explained. The practice ground is the place to hone one's performance whilst waiting for the next 'change game'.

In terms of career planning, an early experience of 'managing change' can be beneficial, in that it will allow the younger manager to question and challenge his/her own beliefs. Too often, the responsibility for managing change occurs when attitudes have become fixed. The practice of mentoring can be encouraged to enable managers to explore the value of conclusions drawn from the management of 'the change challenge' experience.

Table 3.2
Continuous change and adaptation:
A new philosophy of management

Changing management beliefs and attitudes	
Old style	New style
• steady state structures	• dynamic and adaptive organisations
• emphasis on control/reporting	• focus on goal/achievement, devolved authority
• hierarchy and authority	• managers as 'integrators'
• closed/top-down communication	• open 360° communication
• role focus	• goal/strategy focus
• procedures and systems	• process effectiveness/ management
• conformity	• individuality
• reward for length of service	• reward for results
• individual responsibility/ accountability	• team/inter-team working
• risk/change-averse	• continuous challenge and adaptation
• internal focus	• market focus
• top plans/middle co-ordinates/rest deliver	• consensus on strategic direction and plans

Formulating a strategy for change

The other major HR opportunity for raising the 'values in change' debate occurs in the process of planning change.

Developing a shared vision of change

The 'change equation', illustrated in Table 3.3, provides a useful framework for influence. The rationale illustrated is that, for individuals to *want* to change, they need to:

- accept and understand the need for change
- believe that, by changing, a better future will result
- have confidence that they can achieve change
- judge that the benefits through change outweigh the risks of not changing.

If the results of change do not meet such expectations, then individuals will be reluctant to change, expressing such sentiments as:

- 'If change is forced on me, then I will resist it'
- 'Why should I change, as there is nothing in it for me?'
- 'Change means uncertainty and unpredictability. I am not confident that I can adapt or that my boss will support me.'

These fundamental questions and thoughts are at the heart of change thinking. To empower an individual, the responses would need to be:

- 'I believe that, by changing, I will learn and grow and be better able to face up to future challenges'
- 'I have confidence that my boss will allow me to learn from my mistakes'
- 'I believe that our team will pull together and win together.'

For organisational systems – groups or teams rather than individuals – the same criteria apply. The prime difference is that now the need is to develop a critical *mass* of support for and commitment to change. Hence, our challenge is to ensure that managers act as the empowering leaders in change.

The challenge for the Line and the HR functions is to invest in the fostering of this commitment, ownership and energy. Table 3.3 illustrates the 'critical processes' which would allow people to participate in and contribute to change thinking.

A shared vision of change, which embraces the business aim, the positive changes in relationships and the underlying culture, would meet the criteria of empowerment.

If, for example, a business wishes to grow via enhanced New Product Development performance, and this is coupled with a drive to enhance market and customer focus, greater competitive scanning – with teams created to generate ideas and improvements, and management demonstrably ready to listen and learn – then a challenging and beneficial vision will exist. The link between the business need and changing patterns of behaviour and attitudes will be established. The value is that all personnel will be involved in the change process and will strive to create a 'winning team' together. A much more empowering challenge will have been instituted.

Ensuring successful change

The notion of successful change is important. If organisations are intent on making change, how then would they actually monitor achievements? This type of debate can again be empowering, especially if management's aim is to foster commitment and shared ownership. To agree together how we measure success we will need to take account of the different perceptions of the needs for change, and the aspirations of the individuals involved, especially if changing behaviour and relationships are on the agenda.

For the HR professional, such a debate can help in providing an opportunity to challenge aims. As such, empowering values can be added. Table 3.4 demonstrates how the positioning of a change strategy can be effectively achieved. The shift from a

Table 3.3
A strategy for change:
'The change equation'
Key building blocks

Shared ownership of the need for change	+ Common vision of the future	+ Confidence in the feasibility of change	+ Benefits in change	> Risk in not changing
Critical processes				
1 open communication on business issues/concerns	1 clearly articulated goals/success criteria	1 diagnosis of capacity/competence for change	1 balancing financial and people benefits	1 uncontrolled responses, 'knee jerk', reaction
2 involvement in diagnosis of needs for change	2 involvement in planning of change	2 planning change-teams/goals/mileposts/phasing	2 change introduces a new/valued style of management	2 loss of confidence
3 open feedback/challenge to current practices	3 innovation and idea generation	3 active consultation/participation	3 enhances value placed on team/individuals	3 growing fear
4 competitive scanning/benchmarking	4 focus on competitive advantage	4 devolution of responsibilities for success	4 controlled evolution	4 risk/innovation avoidance
5 link between business performance/style/competence/culture	5 valuing individuals and developing relationships	5 focus on organisation rebuilding		5 blaming culture
				6 internal politics

Table 3.4
Success criteria in change

	Business orientation	
	Tactical	Strategic
Organisational perspective	change implementation	competitive advantage and future growth
Individual perspective	individual role clarity and security	individual empowerment and growth

tactical to a strategic perspective on change would be a measure of successful influence.

The stakeholders in change

In our experience, many of the problems with change planning and management are to do with assuming too narrow a perspective on the impact of change. To avoid this, the idea of 'the stakeholders in change' may usefully be considered.

Change can clearly affect the management and staff; but what of our customers, our suppliers, the local community and the City? Tables 3.5 and 3.6 illustrate a process of planning which considers all of the stakeholders in the change context and the potential risks and benefits to each. The proposition of a *'profit and loss response'* to change is thus made.

For a management aiming to empower, this approach would allow all stakeholders to be considered. A stakeholder who has been omitted will draw their own conclusions, probably in terms of being undervalued. Successful change management will require not only a process of communication, but more importantly active consultation and participation.

Table 3.5
The stakeholders in change:
a 'profit and loss' analysis
change means . . . a 'loss' attitude

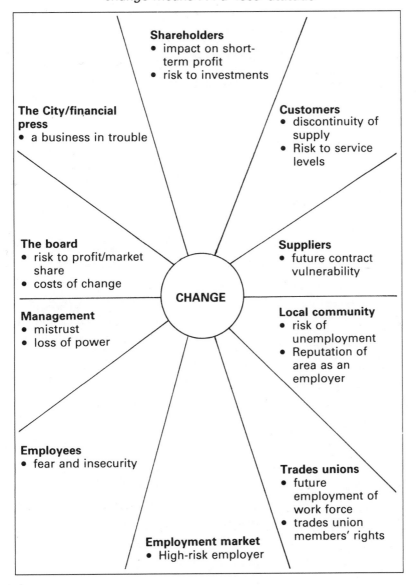

Shareholders
- impact on short-term profit
- risk to investments

The City/financial press
- a business in trouble

Customers
- discontinuity of supply
- Risk to service levels

The board
- risk to profit/market share
- costs of change

CHANGE

Suppliers
- future contract vulnerability

Management
- mistrust
- loss of power

Local community
- risk of unemployment
- Reputation of area as an employer

Employees
- fear and insecurity

Trades unions
- future employment of work force
- trades union members' rights

Employment market
- High-risk employer

Table 3.6
The stakeholders in change:
a 'profit and loss' analysis
change means . . . a 'profit' attitude

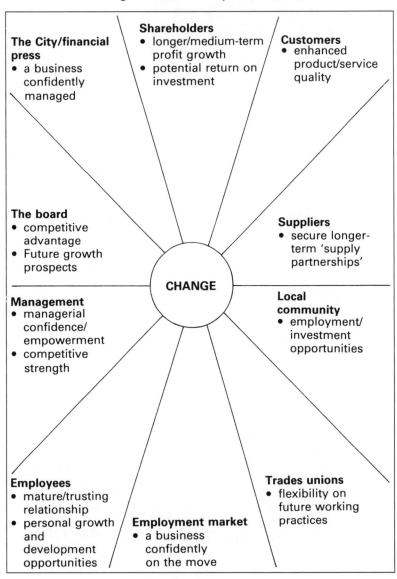

A language of change

This chapter has aimed to create a broad agenda of change considerations. It seems to be clear that successful change will require a new level of thinking and questioning. It also seems that a language for successful change has begun to emerge:

- *'leadership values in change'*
  - Are they 'empowering' or 'devaluing' of the people affected?
- *'a new management philosophy'*
  - Do managers systematically learn about change leadership?
  - What are the underpinning values and assumptions about the effective, adaptive organisation?
  - Are careers planned to equip managers with change leadership experience, skills and values?
- *'formulating a strategy for change'*
  - What plans exist to develop a shared diagnosis and ownership of the need for change?
  - How are people involved in the development of a shared vision of the future which embraces both the business need and the impact on them?
  - How are the benefits in change assessed and sold?
  - What attempts are made to address the 'what's in it for me' need?
- *'defining the success criteria for change'*
  - How are people encouraged to participate in shaping the future?
  - How can successful change momentum be generated and sustained?
  - What plans exist to review and learn together?
- *'delivering a benefit to the stakeholders in change'*
  - What consideration is given to all of the stakeholders in change?
  - Sitting in their shoes, what could be their fears and hopes of change?

- How can we build and extend change partnerships?
- *'the role and influence of HR'*
  - Are we just change facilitators?
  - If we aim to be change partners, what new skills do we need?
  - Are we willing to face management with our own values and beliefs?

4

The HR Function in Transition

From change facilitators to strategic change partners

In the preceding chapters, we have set out an agenda for change for the HR function in terms of its role in the shaping of overall change strategies. Our experience indicates that change strategies are successfully achieved when the HR function is able to position itself as a 'challenging partner' in the overall change process. Our basic proposition regarding 'empowering change' requires a proactive HR function which has sufficient credibility to lead busy line management to address 'empowerment issues'. The issue for many HR directors and their teams is whether they are able, or allowed, to deliver against this challenge.

From the line management perspective, when faced with the challenge of planning major change, the questions are often:

- 'Do we have in place policies and procedures which allow us to make the required changes?'
- 'Are there IR and ER issues that we need to consider which might constrain our freedom of action?'
- 'How open should we be about the need for change?'
- 'How and when should we communicate and consult with staff?'
- 'What facilities do we have in place to protect our reputation as caring and professional employers in terms of redeployment and redundancy?'

The demands and pressures affecting the 'change facilitator' role are substantial in themselves. They are intensified when, as often happens, the HR team finds itself in the *implementation* role in relation to such diverse tasks as:

- facilitating staff communication
- counselling managers and staff
- calculating redundancy and severance pay
- avoiding IR and ER problems
- offering a personal confidential support service to the redeployed and redundant
- participating in management selection decisions
- defining new jobs and their value.

The HR task is both considerable and critical in terms of implementing 'the fair and caring employer' philosophy.

'Why then strive to take on anything more?'

For the HR team this is a fundamental question. If the team perceives its role as that of a custodian of well thought through policies and systems to support change, then the 'change facilitator' role will be wholly congruent. If, however, the team has a genuine commitment to staff, their integrity as human beings, their capacity to face change and be innovative, their willingness to adapt, then the challenge of empowering, enabling and trusting them will emerge. The effect would be to emphasise the HR team's function as 'internal change consultants', advising management on their philosophy and approach to change.

Our notion of the 'strategic change partner' highlights the importance of the early involvement of the HR function in:

- *'formulating strategies for change'*
  with the HR influence being exercised in the planning, as distinct from the implementing, phase

and

- *'acting as a change partner'*
  which assumes that the HR team has established the right to

sit at the 'change planning table' as a partner who will add value to change thinking.

This positioning would ensure that 'empowering change' propositions are addressed earlier rather than later. The risk of addressing them later in the change process is that the focus will then be on:

- the casualties of change
- the manager and his or her new team as they set about rebuilding the organisation
- the repairing and rebuilding of relationships across the organisation.

Prevention can prove less expensive, as well as more prudent, than financing the cure.

This shift will require courage and conviction from the HR team. However, the reputation of HR as a partner in major change processes can in this way be enhanced and its influence more evidently felt.

Traditional and empowering roles

What, then, might be a way of achieving this shift? In Table 4.1, we consider the typical change agenda which businesses are addressing in pursuit of such aims as:

- strategic review and business repositioning
- organisational restructuring and rationalisation
- organisational downsizing and de-layering
- business internationalisation
- performance improvement
- achieving market leadership
- managing acquisitions and mergers

Table 4.1
The HR function in transition

Traditional HR role	Business aim	Empowering HR role
• people implications • HR function as an implementer of change	*Strategic review and business repositioning*	• annual HR audits linked to future business strategies • processes for management/staff communication and consultation • campaigns around corporate mission and values • HR function as a strategic planning partner
• HR policies and procedures facilitate restructuring • counselling and support systems exist • data bases established on current stock of talent	*Organisational restructuring and rationalisation*	• HRD strategy focused on future organisational roles and competences needed • involvement in organisation and job design to ensure role and job challenge

Traditional HR role	Business aim	Empowering HR role
• HR involved in selection decisions • HR acts as staff communicator • HR focuses on the redeployed and redundant	*Organisation restructuring and rationalisation*	• introduce new vision of organisation which enables individuals to grow and develop • career reviews and management focus on individual growth and 'marketability'
• well established redundancy policies and procedures • employee assistance programmes in place • budgets and systems available for career counselling and guidance	*Organisation downsizing and delayering*	• HR policy established and openly communicated on 'no careers for life' • individuals encouraged to take responsibility for own career management • changing employment contracts and benefits to fit with individual mobility and breaking out of 'golden chains' thinking

Table 4.1
continued

Traditional HR role	Business aim	Empowering HR role
• employee communication processes in place • line management support and counselling • Trades Unions agreements exist to enable restructuring processes • HR focus on the 'leavers'	*Organisation downsizing and delayering*	• IT/greater automation strategy linked with HR strategy to avoid unplanned surprises • stress audits and management in place • HR focus on the 'stayers' and the rebuilding of mutual trust and confidence
• policies established to deal with expatriate remuneration and mobility • career management processes exist • counselling/induction for re-deployed staff • all high potential staff expected to have international experience	*Internationalisation*	• HRD strategy linked to future international roles and competencies • career mapping and development established against target competencies • career reviews/mentoring to identify future international cadre • cross-cultural experience and training • family counselling and advice

Traditional HR role	Business aim	Empowering HR role
• staff appraisal and goal setting systems established • management training in coaching and counselling • 'cafeteria'-style reward systems established • incentive schemes • external benchmarking of reward schemes • 'hire and fire' philosophy • suggestion schemes	*Performance improvement*	• OD strategies aimed at creating 'high performance cultures' • HRD policies and plans targeted towards high performance competencies • regular attitude/climate surveys • leadership style and behaviour training • policies and practices regularly challenged and reviewed • team based reward systems • attractive bonus/incentive schemes • open communication encouraged • 360 degree feedbacks on performance and individual development

Table 4.1
continued

Traditional HR role	Business aim	Empowering HR role
• customer service campaigns • review of compensation and benefit packages • recruitment policies and practices • internal selection and promotion processes • career management systems • headhunting facility established • networks exist with leading academic institutions	*Market leadership*	• reviewing competitive behaviour and benchmarking quality of staff • HR policies geared to support NPD, innovation and change management • linking business strategy to HRD strategy • HRD geared to 'leading marketing, sales and R&D competencies' • communication of business focus and priorities on customer/market orientation • task forces on critical market leadership issues • OD exercises on 'market/customer focus' and the culture needed

Traditional HR role	Business aim	Empowering HR role
• HR involved 'after the event' to review compatibility of HR policies and practices	*Acquisitions and mergers*	• early involvement of HR in planning screening of acquisition candidates
• acquired staff communication and induction programmes		• education of directors/ management in 'the cultural fit' issues
• management team introduced to manage synergies and integration		• developing new identity and values within newly constituted companies
		• ensuring people and culture issues are given a value equal to commercial and financial issues
		• carrying out 'culture fit' audits
		• identifying and selecting managers who are skilled in 'merger management' and who can empathise with the needs of the 'incomers'
		• HRD strategy focuses on building a cadre of highly competent managers who can deal with mergers, acquisitions and joint ventures

The data illustrates potential differences between 'traditional' and 'empowering' HR activities.

A range of concepts emerge from this analysis which demonstrate the 'strategic partner' role:

- **HR audits**
  these examine the capacity of the people system and the organisational culture to deliver strategic ambition
- **future organisational options and the competences needed**
  these focus HRD thinking on the future business needs
- **individual responsibility for growth and future career**
  this shifts the emphasis from the 'paternalistic/dependency' thinking towards 'mature inter-dependency' around future career direction
- **stress audits**
  these confront the real risk in today's organisational life of high pressure and ambiguity
- **career challenge planning**
  this emphasises that individual growth experience needs to be focused on the competences and experience sought for future roles
- **team based reward**
  this regards teamworking and cross-team collaboration as prerequisites to developing a creative and responsive organisation
- **culture change**
  this recognises that organisational culture and behaviour can either help or hinder change.

All of these factors demonstrate a focus on future planning and emphasise the importance of individual, team and organisational growth and empowerment.

For the strategically orientated HR team, these (and other) initiatives would become the order of the day, with the result that less time would be spent on the maintenance of the status quo and operational day to day thinking. The question would centre upon the true 'added value' role for HR. A major campaign, aimed at challenging the impact of existing policies, practices and procedures on organisational responsiveness and

Table 4.2
The changing role of personnel

Away from	→Towards
• custodians of 'good' personnel management practices	• strategic partners
• definition of HR policies and procedures	• enabling policies and practices
• experts in personnel management matters	• handing over HR activities to the line
• counselling managers and staff	• challenging and trusted partners
• developing and training individuals and teams	• individual responsibility for own growth development and future careers
• caring and supporting	• empowering
Personnel management	→Internal HR consultancy

performance, would be required to bring about the desired empowered partnership.

Table 4.2 illustrates the typical changes involved in the transition in status from expert in 'personnel management' systems and practices to that of autonomous 'internal HR consultant'. Consultancy implies the ability to demonstrate 'added value' advice and service against specific projects and interventions. Many companies are witnessing this shift, which realigns the HR and other staff functions (eg finance, IT, management services) as cost centres selling their services, and, as such, agents for establishing 'high performance' and 'cost effective' organisational culture.

Influence mapping

The ability of the HR team to achieve these shifts will depend substantially on the 'true' level of influence exerted. Here, an

honest questioning and re-appraisal will be needed. The
capacity for assessing the scope and influence of HR is
fundamental to meeting the 'empowering challenge'.

Table 4.3 introduces the notion of 'influence mapping'. The
matrix illustrated has dual dimensions of

- *'level of influence'*
  which starts at the HR team, to ensure that all members are
  committed to the more proactive and challenging role, from
  individual employees right through to Board level

and

- *'influence on the change agenda'*
  which embraces scanning and anticipating the need for
  change, as well as exerting influence on the change strategies,
  through to instituting change as normal practice.

The notion of mapping may be used by HR teams to sketch out
the existing boundaries of their influence and then to set
themselves a 'change strategy', which will shift them towards
the role and influence sought. An interesting exercise here
would be to compare and contrast this with the line management – 'client' – perspective.

The elements of the 'change agenda' illustrated are typical
phases in the overall change process. For example:

- *scanning and anticipating* could involve changes in the
  employment market place, benchmarking against competitors, as well as being aware of the overall business strategy
  and assessing the capacity of the people organisation and
  culture to deliver
- *envisioning the future* integrates both the business aim and
  the changes in culture and organisational behaviour needed
- *process design* would examine the 'critical success factors' in

Table 4.3

The role and scope of HR influence mapping

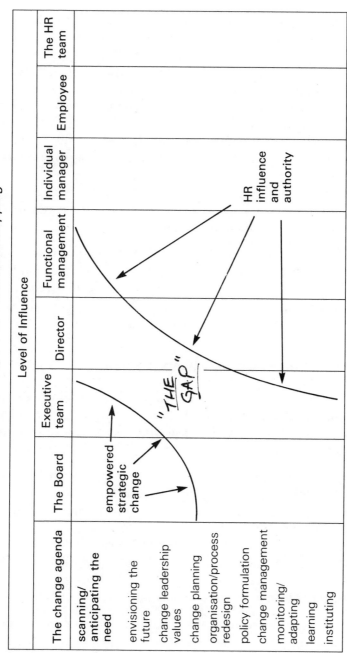

the businesses, eg NPD, customer service, supply chain
management, and the processes needed
- *job/work redesign* would explore the challenges and motivations with the new job and teamworking/flexible working
- *monitoring and adapting* would review the impact of change
  and conceive of initiatives needed to sustain the change
  focus and momentum
- *learning* would question the lessons learnt about change
  management, and investigate the learning needed to establish the new style of operation
- *instituting* emphasises the need to integrate change into the
  normal, on-going, processes of goal setting, reward, career
  and individual development.

HR teams would need to ensure that they possessed this array
of competences in their 'change repertoire': their added value
as 'internal change consultants' would be delivered from this
influence base.

Facing the emerging change agenda

A 'hearts and minds' review for the HR professionals involved
will be required if this challenge is to be realistically faced.
Risks invariably attend upon change, and, those that may well
surface here include:

- the risk that line management may want a responsive and
  facilitative team of a more traditional style
- the risk that the HR team itself may not wish to or feel
  capable of change
- the risk that to question the HR team's values may give rise
  to still further questions about traditional thinking and
  practices
- the risk that the sought for influence may not be attained.

The question perhaps should address the consequences of *not*
facing up to the challenge, and of *not* dealing with the risks

Table 4.4
The change challenge
The HR function in transition

		HR role in change	
		Traditional	Empowering
Change	Organisation	facilitating change	challenging strategic partner
Values	Individual	informing educating counselling adaptation	empowering releasing creativity and innovation self-determination

involved. It is often said, that organisations 'establish the HR team they deserve'. HR needs to be, and be seen to be, a role model of 'a responsive and adaptive organisation'. Their credibility in giving advice to the line would be much enhanced by living the sought for values in practice. These are illustrated in Table 4.4.

For the *empowering HR team*, key questions would include:

- 'What values do we hold important to successful change mangement?'
- 'What challenges would we need to raise with the line?'
- 'Where are we now in terms of HR function?'
- 'What do we need to do "to put our own house in order"?'
- 'Where would we wish to be in terms of our role and influence?'
- 'Who are the key players who can affect our plans?'
- 'What credibility and influence do we have with them?'
- 'What new competences and skills will we need?'
- 'How do we plan to work together as a team moving into the future?'

In the final chapter, we further explore the vision of HR as 'a Strategic Partner'.

5

▰ Managing Restructuring – A Case Study

An era of restructuring

Restructuring and rationalisation are the currency of management thinking about change in the 1990s. The emerging business environment can be characterised as a continuous search for ways of:

- sustaining profit growth when faced with tough competition and pressure on the price of goods and services
- investing in the upgrading of product and service quality and of customer service
- focusing management energy on new market opportunities
- quickening responsiveness to market change
- accelerating the delivery of new products and services against a backdrop of shorter product life cycles
- challenging internal cost structures and the price of bureaucracy.

These, and other, challenges – which aim to squeeze more out of today's operations to invest into tomorrow's business – raise a major leadership and motivational problem. The drive for efficiency and cost saving will throw a spotlight on opportunities for greater automation, flexible working practices, challenges to bureaucracy, and reduction of management levels and people costs.

This drive for saving will be replicated in re-negotiating costs with suppliers and distributors. 'Just in time' thinking is a visible example of suppliers carrying the stockholding and distribution costs. This cycle of tough commercial relationships heightens the levels of risk and uncertainty felt. Unfortunately, in terms of this model, everyone in the supply chain is either somebody's 'supplier' or 'customer'. There is and will be no respite from this quest and the style of relationship it inspires, either within or outside of our various business enterprises.

The question is whether this overall process of change is empowering or disempowering. The argument often used is that, in hard times, tough action is needed. In an era of benefit/cost thinking, it is, however, worth standing back to assess restructuring against those variables. In Table 5.1, a potential balance sheet is drawn.

A major issue is that restructuring has become the norm – a basis for change management behaviour which is based on a 'take it or leave it' philosophy. People and their experience are increasingly perceived as disposable commodities. People have long memories, however, and the essence of the trusting relationship between employer and employee can be eroded and destroyed by such an attitude. In Chapter 11, we further enlarge on the risk to trust.

In our experience, the restructuring philosophy occasionally runs the risk of turning into a 'knee jerk' response. The attitude implied by asking, 'what is the benefit of moving the deckchairs on the Titanic?' can too readily become entrenched. Organisational sceptics are quick to justify and develop this line of argument. These champions of doubt within companies can become the opinion formers around whom a dubious rationale for management behaviour in change can be drawn. Even though management's aim may be to refocus, simplify, and unclutter, what results may be heightened suspicion and mistrust. People's instincts become highly sensitised, whatever the bosses' stated intent and overt behaviour, in prolonged periods of change and turmoil. The problem is that the conclusions are often drawn from individual perceptions, which are based on their own values, around how they would wish to be treated by bosses. Perceptions are personally held views and feelings which can too readily become facts. Any leader of change who neglects the damaging potential of mistrustful emplolyees runs the risk of

Table 5.1
A case for restructuring
A cost/benefit analysis

	Benefits	Costs

economic	efficiency savings and tighter business focus
	
	organisational simplification
	
	improved ratios
	– overhead costs
	– costs of sales
	
	tighter supply chain management, and short term profit performance
		costs of restructuring
		– redundancy
		  redeployment
		  closure
		
		market image and reputation
		
		reduced investment into the future
		– R&D
		– NPD
		
		supplier relationships

people	organisational shake up clears out the under performers clearer accountabilities established reward for results philosophy established being selected and surviving	'start up' time of new structure heightened levels of personal risk risk and challenge avoidance, low innovation levels employment and career contract dislocated

being perceived as valueless. Our proposition of 'empowerment through change' is the gauntlet that such management still needs to pick up.

The following case studies from **Shell International** aim to illustrate how a company, faced with the need for radical structural change, was able to work towards a strategy of re-empowerment.

A Shell International case study of structural change

The need for change – a history

In 1956, the Royal Dutch Shell Group of Companies invested in a major petrochemical complex. The acquisition was to become part of one of the largest downstream developments of any oil major. By 1981, the chemical interests accounted for some 10 per cent of the Shell Companies' turnover, and RDSG was ranked as the eighth largest chemical company in the world, with proceeds of over £3,000 million.

In the 1960s, the growth of the Shell Companies' Chemical business, although rapid, was paralleled by similar growth in many competitor organisations, as companies sought to take advantage of a world market growing at 15 per cent per annum with little change forecast. Programmes to build more capacity were established by the industry in most of the developed countries.

During this period, an empowering philosophy was established. Confidence in the business future enabled management to invest in people. A major exercise of establishing a high performance, future oriented, culture was instituted. Organisational and cultural development was planned. A philosophy of 'people and culture matter' was adopted, and a period of expansion was underway.

Then came the first oil crisis in 1973, and the future was rewritten. Forecasts of growth rates were halved, only subsequently to be halved and halved again. By the end of the decade, the industrial face of the world had significantly changed and the international petrochemical business, founded and build on double figure annual growth rates, was in a state of disarray. Over-production, with demand remaining at 60 per cent below capacity, uneconomic plant utilisation, tumbling prices and astronomic losses demanded radical responses, at industry and company levels.

The risks of breaking an organisational culture with a tradition related to growth were, however, all too apparent. At the time when losses were beginning to hit operating companies, the process of evolutionary adaptation, using OD thinking, was underway in those Shell Service Companies, the joint Head offices, concerned with the international chemical business (London and The Hague). Progress had been patchy, though, and some managers were beginning to 'go it alone', introducing radical changes in procedures and methods in response to growing business pressures to rationalise products, plants and services.

Should this be encouraged? If so, how could cohesion and consistency be maintained? Some managers, feeling the constraints of the conservative, evolutionary approach, advocated a complete change from the centralised approach to a decentralised mode, in an attempt to reduce overheads and give more flexibility to the local operating companies. Would such a radical switch be possible? Could commitment be developed rapidly? Would resistance to imposed change and internal conflict slow down progress? These were some of the issues that faced the leadership as the business pressures mounted.

The aims of change – senior management's view

The coincidence of the needs for urgent business rationalisation and for a co-ordinated, cohesive approach to change meant that a choice was required – either to persist with evolution or else to impose change because of the urgency of the situation. In the event a middle course was chosen: namely, to have an organisation study carried out under the direction of the top management team, and then to use the proposed reorganisation as the vehicle for change.

The recommendations were that, with low growth prospects, the Operating Companies should be freed to respond as far as possible to local market conditions – whilst not threatening the optimisation of Shell Companies' business – with the Service Companies re-aligning their roles to focus on long-term prospects and strategies.

The existing organisation had been product based, with

business strategies being co-ordinated centrally with Operating Companies' input (see Figure 5.1).

To achieve this distinction of roles, the study emphasised that any change of structure should have the following aims:

- to improve co-ordination against overall strategies
- to create clearer accountability within and between the Service Companies and Operating Companies
- to reduce the involvement of the Service Companies in the Operating Companies' ongoing chemicals operations
- to improve mechanisms for conflict resolution across the sector
- to increase emphasis on advice and services from Service Companies to Operating companies.

These aims reflected the need to change the Service Company role and its relationship with the Operating Companies. They represented a clear challenge to the traditional Service Company activity: to become more strategic and less involved in the day-to-day optimisation of the business – a breaking of the implicit power base, to be paralleled with a run down of the Central Office staff of some 20 per cent. The revolution had begun! The changes implied would significantly affect all of Shell Companies' Chemical business, with a turnover of £3 billion and over 50 Operating Companies covering a world-wide market. Figures 5.1 and 5.2 illustrate the scale of the planned structural changes.

The sector was run on a matrix principle, in which functions and locations were represented in 'business groups'. This structural device had attempted to create an integrated business process in which all the parties contributed, through the matrix and by placing the emphasis on functional activity. Thus, for example, 'manufacturing was to manufacture' and not become involved in long business co-ordination debates; trading was to be broken out from the business units, and given a new and separate identity; and strategic planning was to be co-ordinated for the whole of the petrochemicals business.

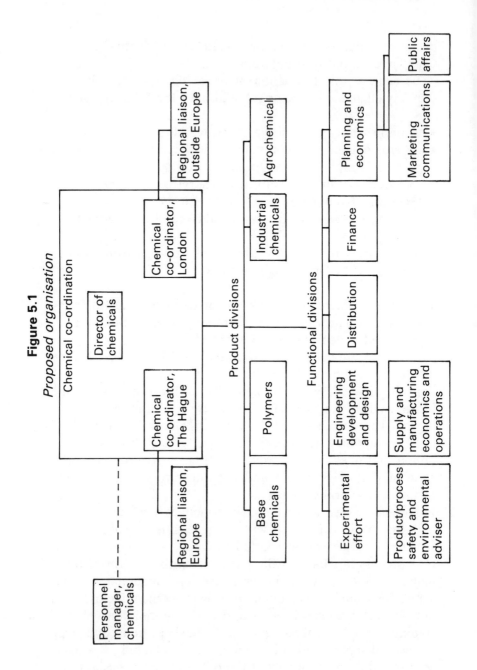

Figure 5.1
Proposed organisation

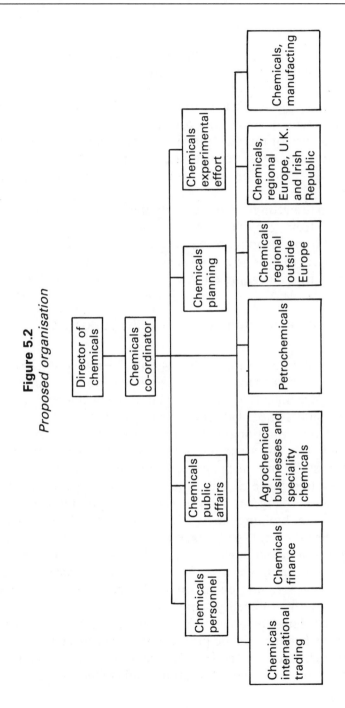

Figure 5.2
Proposed organisation

The overall shift within the Service Companies was toward the provision of service to Operating Companies and toward the representation of the shareholders in these operating companies. It is interesting to note that the capacity to change to a new type of organisation was embedded in the principles and structure of the old organisation. To move to a decentralised structure would require careful central co-ordination. To make the revolution work an evolutionary approach was needed.

The battleground was defined: the need for a change of strategy from growth to retrenchment; to establish a new leadership philosophy; to devolve the organisation; to reduce manpower; to change attitudes and responses; and, of course, while all this was going on, the business still had to be run.

Evolution or revolution – the challenge to HR

What should be the role of HR within this revolution? Should it carry on as in the past or shift to a new mode of operation?

HR in Chemicals had been linked to the development of the matrix, and hence was 'traditional', in that it attempted to support an evolutionary development mode. The HR work proceeded on the assumption that creation of the appropriate culture, skills and mechanisms would engender the capacities required to achieve change. The approach was patient, consultative and emergent, and succeeded in providing a set of fundamental building blocks which, during the 1970s, enabled many developments to be tackled successfully. The emphasis was on product strategies, project development, and bottom-up policy forming via cross-functional teams, processes which were very relevant to evolutionary change – yet, in retrospect, inadequate for radical system change.

This challenge of an evolutionary or a revolutionary response to change again raises the problem of delivering empowerment through change. For the HR OD team involved, the issue was whether to join the revolution and influence leadership

Table 5.2
Evolution versus revolution in change

Evolution	Revolution
'Evolution is not a force but a process, not a cause but a law' (Morley, 1874)	'Revolution is not a dinner party . . . it cannot be so leisurely and gentle . . . A revolution is an insurrection, an act of violence . . .' (Mao Tse-tung, 1927)
Evolutionary change: • follows laws • is slow • results in casualties • is environmentally determined	Revolutionary change: • breaks laws • is rapid • results in casualties • breaks constraints
Traditional HR values: • searching for order • planning change • valuing individuals • emphasising learning	Today's business needs: • to survive • to respond rapidly • to value contribution • to emphasise capability

thinking on the run or whether to adopt a more conservative strategy. The latter alternative would involve assuming the traditional HR role of caring for the re-deployed and redundant, managing the ER implications, and helping in the resourcing decisions for the new organisation. The nature of the choice is set out in Table 5.2.

The choice was made to join the revolution and to adopt an opportunistic challenging philosophy.

The leadership challenge – facing the complexities of change

The complexity of the issues to be faced in the required restructuring of Shell's Chemicals business resulted in an unprecedented level of internal tension. Longer term business interests – the need to maintain adequate levels of investment – conflicted with the short term needs for positive cash flow. Healthy sectors of the business, in particular the Speciality

Chemicals and other higher added value activities, conflicted with those sectors which were in decline, and fought to maintain distance between themselves and the troubled businesses in an attempt to differentiate their structures and approaches.

Functions conflicted over which way the battle should be fought and where savings should be made. Individuals conflicted as the competition for personal survival increased. Externally, the market-place became a battle ground on which new allegiances were forged, as companies struggled to survive. At the leadership level in the Service Companies, the conflict focused initially on the change management style to be adopted. A rapid response was required, yet most of the organisation's leaders had been associated with gradual development strategies spanning years rather than weeks. The service organisations housed the business leaders in terms of professional expertise and international business experience. These high quality, high level staff were used to a full involvement in organisational and business matters. The apparent imposition of 'an organisation' was an act which might have been seen to cut across the culture of an organisation which traditionally had stressed involvement and participation at all levels.

In addition, the various chemical businesses comprising the biggest part of the service organisations had been run on semi-autonomous lines, with differences in business and management approach being reflected in the structures and procedures. To apply uniform standards across the whole business spectrum was felt by many to put at risk some of the unique skills of these distinctive business approaches.

Also at risk were people. A large number of volunteers for early retirement would be needed, and a larger number required for redeployment in other parts of the Shell Group, if the overall objectives were to be met. In order to improve the chances of redeployment, a large pool of staff was offered for transfer. Although this increased the chance of successful selection, it also increased the number of people faced with uncertainty.

Table 5.3

Leadership choice – what style can or should we adopt?

Evolution – let it happen?	[or] *Revolution* – make it happen?
Risks • piecemeal evolution • pockets of revolution • varying levels of awareness of need • varying levels of commitment to manage change • failure due to slow response	**Risks** • breaking traditional norms • top-down change imposed with the same top team in place • change could be perceived as lacking confidence in staff • solution may not be supported by all • leadership would need to take risks and inevitably be under close scrutiny
Benefits • consultation would lead to commitment and understanding • demonstration of value placed on knowledge and experience • new organisation soundly appraised at planning stage • opportunity for building new relationships	**Benefits** • sense of urgency would be apparent • shake-up could result in questioning of old attitudes/ approach • top management commitment to change would be demonstrated • early achievements in making change could provide a confident basis for next steps

Finally, there was no consistency of commitment to change. Some line managers felt that their organisations were capable of meeting the challenge, while others believed that radical change was just what was required. Table 5.3 illustrates the complexities of the choice facing the leadership.

Formulating an enabling strategy

Against the scale of challenges envisaged and backed by an 'empowering' philosophy, a plan was established which embraced an array on initiatives:

- communication
- re-training
- organisational re-definition
- staff support systems
- review processes

The components and dynamics of this 'enabling strategy' are illustrated in Figure 5.3.

With an unknown number of staff about to lose their jobs (in the event a reduction of 25 per cent in job stock was achieved), and with the bulk of the Service Company roles being changed, the priority was to gear up to handle the displaced staff in as humane, responsible and professional a manner as possible.

Communication to staff in a multinational organisation is never easy. In this case, the difficulty was compounded by having major groups based in London and The Hague, in addition to many staff on secondment to Shell Operating Companies around the world (some 50 companies both wholly and jointly owned). It was agreed that senior management should give formal presentations in London and The Hague; the same text and the same handout material would be sent to all Chemicals-based staff around the world. The presentations took place in the Companies' theatres to audiences of 300 plus. The HR team contributed to the design of the presentation, which dealt with:

- the state of the business
- the aims of the changes
- new structure
- implementation plans
- staff issues
- questions and discussion.

These public sessions clearly confirmed staff fears, but, as is usual in such large gatherings, most concerns remained unvoiced. The frustration and the dismay had to be dealt with by the individual members of the management team. At this level, questions emerged about:

OD team's enabling strategy: components and dynamics

Enabling Strategy

Establish top management group as a steering group for the overall change process

Create a common vision and establish a change plan

System's capability to learn and adapt

Need for change/ planned restructuring

ACTION

COMMUNICATION

Announcement

Repeat series of discussions

Communicate regularly

ORGANISATION DEFINITION

Define roles and job groupings' responsibilities

Continue this process downwards

Work on inter-relationships between groups internally

Work on inter-relationships between centres and environments

NEW SYSTEMS

Special studies

Information, technology and requirements

New information flows

STAFF SELECTION AND SUPPORT

Managing staff changes

Life planning counselling

Re-training

REVIEW

Revisit overall vision regularly

Reviewing mechanism listening feedback

RE-TRAINING

Identify and initiate development of skills

Role definition diagnose skills

Development courses/ workshops

Table 5.4

Conflicts in change

New line management aims	HR aims	Staff needs
• to get on with implementation	• to create a 'felt fair' system for dealing with staff	• to reduce uncertainty but still adhere to the voluntary severance scheme
• to secure their own divisions and the best staff possible	• to maintain consistency across divisions	• to understand the direction of the changes
• to design and implement new organisations	• to apply the rules fairly	• to ensure open management
• to minimise the business risk	• to ensure the use of staff consultation machinery	• to be involved in the design work
• to keep their staff plans confidential but deal fairly with the staff	• to achieve redeployment of all staff displaced	• to contribute to the decision making
Resulting in feelings of:		
• frustration	• isolation	• ambiguity
• anxiety	• blame	• uncertainty
• responsibility	• overload	• fear
• challenge	• defensiveness	• betrayal

- the validity of the new organisation in light of the needs of the European Chemical business for central co-ordination
- the 'sell out' of past beliefs by senior management
- the staff selection processes.

The battleground was now visible, the management team was under attack and some were feeling vulnerable. Table 5.4 illustrates the potential 'conflicts'.

Table 5.5
Review timetable

Months into implementation	Anticipated focus of review	Data-gathering
1 (Initial)	leadership performance	from members of team
4 (Interim)	team cohesion, common understanding and divisional progress	from members of team and next level down
10 (Year end)	total sector implications and critical interfaces	total Chemicals sector

Re-empowering through review

The resultant enabling plan provided an opportunity for the HR and management teams to take stock. The original concerns about a revolutionary versus an evolutionary approach were being confirmed. There was a clear need for an overall change plan. Demands for coherent consistency within the top management team were being made, and the value of regular reviews was established as the basis for shifting the balance from 'revolutionary' to 'evolutionary' thinking. The focus of these reviews was to be aimed sequentially at:

- the leadership of the change process
- the Divisional 'pick up' of the change philosophy
- the impact on the overall sector of new organisational philosophy in practice

Table 5.5 illustrates the review timetable.

The initial review was carried out by the HR OD team, interviewing the top team on their views of the overall leadership of change performance. Table 5.6 illustrates the issues raised.

Leadership style proved to be a priority issue – the pressure for team cohesion being apparent – and yet doubts about the overall direction still prevailed, particularly in the context of

Table 5.6
Initial review lessons

- lack of listening
- low valuing of each other
- limited trust and mutual respect
- divisive polarising of issues
- no challenge/risk taking
- superficial co-operation
- lack of structure and meeting disciplines
- consisting of individuals who succeeded within the previous organisation philosophy
- coming out of a difficult and demanding period with widely varying aims
- being pressurised to address significant and difficult strategic issues

the business which has to be carried out 'as usual', in a difficult economic climate. This emphasis on team cohesion reflected clearly the impact on senior management of a period of high uncertainty and conflicting demands. The business required speedy reactions, rapid transactions, and minimal disturbance, while the described reorganisation strategy, which included the lengthy voluntary severance scheme, required a slow transformation. The concept of evolution is easier to hold in balance in the mind rather than in practice. The situation was recognised, but the pressures on management were still associated with task and getting things done. Thus, although process problems were now 'on the table', the focus was still on task. It was not until the third review, 10 months after implementation, that the team faced up to the issues which are given in Table 5.6.

The HR OD team's aim was to adopt a learning and challenging position, in an attempt to ensure that values and behaviour in change were publicly addressed. In planning and review meetings, the debate centred around the gaps between the 'desired' and 'unplanned' consequences of the 'enforced revolution'. The team was determined to hold this mirror up to management to challenge the difference between real be-

Table 5.7
Two views of the change experience

Desired (evolution)	Actual (revolution)	
• agreeing on the need for change	• the business need	⎧ prescribed
	• people's need	⎨ unco-ordinated
		⎩ conflicting
• building a common vision of the future	• primary effort into gaining acceptance of new organisation	
• agreeing and communicating the underlying goals of change	• consultation and running of the business inhibited by constraints of voluntary severance scheme	
• achieving planned change	• primary effort into following personnel guidelines	
• agreeing on a consistent leadership approach	• limited discussion on communication plan	
• gaining commitment and understanding	• parochial quick selling with mixed quality of consultation down the line	
• implementing in a consistent manner	• very limited cohesion	
• reviewing progress and building our capacity to manage change and plan for improvement based on experience and learning	• reviews planned but not implemented	
• learning and improving	• no attempt to learn	

haviour and practice and theory. Table 5.7 illustrates these insights. This challenge, although clearly recognised, was seen as being uncomfortable and inappropriate.

As expected, a counter-argument was developed by the management, whose outlook is summarised in Table 5.8. The challenge had been made and the seeds of doubt sown.

Table 5.8
Management perspectives

---

1. *Environment*
   There is a growing number of discrepancies between our
   developing understanding of our role and environmental
   expectation. Insufficient effort is being dedicated to creating a
   better match.

2. *Strengths*
   The organisation is settling down well, and the anticipated
   advantages are beginning to show. Success is being attributed
   to quality of staff rather than quality of vision.

3. *Weaknesses*
   Most deficiencies are attributable to the newness of the
   operation. Given time, and a commitment to monitor and tune
   the organisation, the weaknesses can be overcome.

4. *Opportunities*
   The important oportunities are at the interface with operating
   companies and industry. Currently, our energies are directed
   at systems and procedures and internal operations.

The interim review was held four months after the establishment of the new organisation. Building on the experience of
the first review, in which some of the contentious issues raised
had been challenged, a more systematic approach was
followed. The HR OD team set out to gather data from all
divisions and functions. The data gathered (Table 5.9) reinforced the challenge to the leadership of the restructuring
process. This time, the top team accepted the challenge and
determined to address the issues raised.

The year end review, which evaluated the process of change,
resulted in the plan to gather data from across the whole of the
Chemicals Sector (see Figure 5.4). In this review, the HR team
set themselves the goals of:

- transferring responsibility to the line to review progress and
  learn, and
- shifting emphasis from reviewing organisational change to

Figure 5.4

The chemicals sector at Royal Dutch Shell

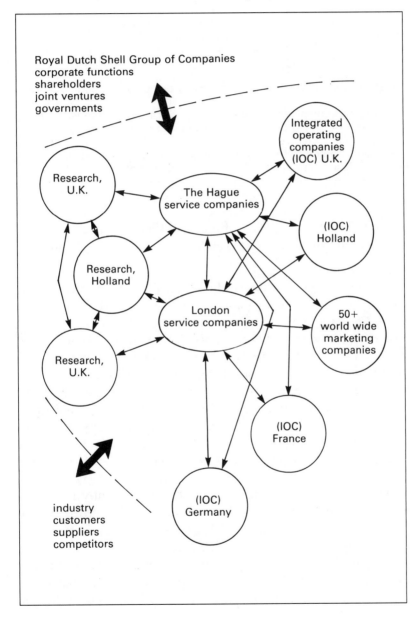

Table 5.9
Pockets of resistance and barriers to progress

- mixed commitment to viability of new approach
- management giving mixed messages
- far too much on management's plate
- people still trying to do old things/ haven't grasped the significance of change
- leadership vacillating between an autocratic and a participatory style
- whole Chemical sector needs to be educated on changes which affect not only the cental organisation, but the operating companies themselves
- black and white thinking in addressing crucial grey areas, especially with regard to operational implications of overall vision

considering the capacity of the total sector to plan and adapt to the major business rationalisation challenges ahead.

The first point was to be only partially achieved, since senior management wished to maintain the services of the HR OD team in data gathering and synthesis. The review was to embrace the views of the Service Companies, in The Hague and in London, together with 13 Operating Companies scattered around the world (see Table 5.10). This in itself provided a major co-ordination and logistics challenge to the team. Extra OD consultants were co-opted, a data gathering timetable established, and a series of off-site sessions set up to assimilate and synthesise the data. The need to achieve consistency in data gathering was paramount, and once again a questionnaire-type approach was adopted.

The focus of this review was to be action centred and not retrospective. After one year, the emphasis had to be on the way ahead. The criteria used for measuring success were the original aims of change (see Table 5.11).

All of the participating companies were briefed on the overall assessment and the sectors plan for the way ahead. A new consensus was beginning to emerge. The critical outcome

Table 5.10

Countries involved in year end review

• United Kingdom	• Spain
• Holland	• Switzerland
• France	• Brazil
• Germany	• South Africa
• Norway	• Japan
• Italy	• Australia
• Portugal	

was that, even after such a major revolution, a new focus and direction was emerging. Key successes identified were:

- the Chemical Sector had established an integrated strategy for the total world wide business
- a leaner, more efficient, service company structure was in place
- the managers of the organisation had built up a substantial store of change management knowledge
- the leaders had gained confidence in their ability to manage a major 'revolution', but had also recognised that different leadership options were both needed and available.

These changes are the spoils of revolution, but they were not gained without cost.

Table 5.11

Year end review

Original aims of change	Example of progress	Typical emerging issues
development of integrated strategies	• major or strategic issues identified • new strategy development methodology providing common language across business	• strategy implemented presenting a new challenge • co-ordinating and intergrating meetings needing wider representation
integrated approach to business appraisal and development	• positive response from Operating Companies • improved planning cycle meshing with business processes	• appraisal function is under-resourced • information requirements
separate central trading identity	• improved market discipline • growing expertise and a focus for a third party supply	• dichotomy between short and long term market objectives • higher market visibility required
strengthening of service and advisory role	• focus on cost savings and efficiency seen as highly valuable	• an information vacuum developing between manufacturing and marketing oriented functions
improved mechanism for conflict resolution	• time being invested across boundaries • staff communication meetings developing well	• short term conflict resolution mechanisms still absent eg product pricing

Table 5.12

The process of rationalisation

the strategic review phase	key issues
• the **why** of change	– competitive pressure – strategic review – re-assessment of corporate identity and mission – review of the organisation
the planning phase	
• the **what** of change	– change leadership philosophy – the objectives of change – management roles and responsibilities in the new organisation – the selection process – the redeployment and support philosophy
the organisation 'start up' process	
• the **how** of change	– allocating responsibilities – training in new competences – new team building – goal agreement – interface definition – the MIS needed – the performance management philosophy
the change implementation process	
• the **results** of change	– regular review/ feedback – drawing out the lessons – achieving results – out-performing the competition

Lessons on rationalisation and restructuring

At the beginning of this chapter, we drew up a cost/benefit analysis of the risks of major restructuring and rationalisation. The key lesson would appear to be that eventually a revolution can be turned into a process of evolution, if regular reviews and systematic feedback are put in place which are positively and openly considered. This learning cycle of action, feedback and drawing out the lessons is an essential part of our empowering philosophy.

More specific lessons emerging are:

- *Rebuilding needs to start once the revolution has begun*
  To perceive rationalisation as a discrete finite step which, when finished, would be followed by a rebuilding process, is a mistake. To delay is to devalue the role and potential of people in contributing to change. The model illustrated in Table 5.12 indicates the typical phases of any process of rationalisation. This model indicates the different levels at which management can target their 'empowerment' philosophy.
- *The way change is managed becomes the new leadership philosophy in practice*
  Change, as we have described before, sensitises both managers and staff. Leadership behaviour is critically observed and scrutinised. No matter what is said about a change philosophy, their actions and behaviour are the critical test of true managerial values in practice.
- *Fragmentation is inevitable*
  Different managers have different leadership philosophies and approaches. Whatever commitments are made on cabinet loyalty, managers will still act against their view of what is best for their part of the business and their people. The lesson here is that there is a need for HR
  – to offer one to one Director level counselling, and
  – to establish a team basis for regular and open feedback.
  The aim of any change process should not be to pigeon-hole management behaviour, but to release individual empowering aproaches, provided this is in line with a common set of team values and a shared philosophy.
- *Change planning is a priority*
  Planning provides the opportunity to consider the different change philosophies and approaches needed. The setting of

clear change goals provides not only the focus for change but also the criteria for structured reviews.

- *Revolutions are not always bad*
  Many HR people would prefer an approach based on continuous evolution. Our case study, however, surely illustrates that a revolution, coupled with challenging reviews, can raise the critical issues to do with successful change management. The pressure for action will demand that the lessons drawn on the run will need to be based on well argued values. As such, those taken on board will be seen to be critical, and will persist with management through time and equip them for their next change challenge.
- *HR teams need the courage of their own convictions*
  The opportunistic philosophy adopted placed great demands on the HR change support team. It would have been too easy for them to adopt a facilitative role. To cause senior management to regularly stop and take stock, and also to challenge them on their approaches, required courage, broad change knowledge and experience, and, most importantly, a real commitment to 'empowering values'.

In this case study, courage resulted in an enforced and needed revolution which was systematically converted to a learning based evolution.

6

▉ Internationalising Business – A Case Study

Many businesses have taken the decision to develop outside the UK. The process of growth may be by:

- ventures with others
- acquisition
- mergers
- organic growth.

Whichever option a company takes will have a significant influence on the role of the HR professionals involved.

The contours of the HR function will remain roughly the same. Professionals are likely to continue to work on selection, training, compensation and benefits, counselling, manpower planning and employee relations tasks. Each of these work areas will, however, be affected in some measure by the number of people who are employed; and, as the number of countries and continents operated in increases, so the range and nature of the problems faced by the HR professional will also increase. The process of geographical dispersion will undoubtedly have an impact on the HR professional who seeks to influence staff in many places, not only in the UK, but around the globe. The expansion of a company internationally can give rise to the need to adopt a role model for the HR professional which is commensurate with new international, even global, perspectives and responsibilities.

Models for the international HR role

The HR professional could adopt the role of *global company policeman*. S/he could seek to draw up guidelines for all the conceivable actions in relation to HR matters which managers could face, and then, by close monitoring, ensure that they are complied with. This was the model adopted by many USA-based companies as they expanded globally. The HR manager thus becomes the person who writes the corporate bible, and then, when required, interprets its meaning for any manager's particular actions. Such HR managers spend considerable time advising senior line managers on such issues as the financial package for particular staff relocating to other countries; the kind of car that is 'allowed' at specific grades in particular countries; allowances for children's education in exotic locations; and even 'in house' case law on the cost of flying a partner back to the UK where a baby needs care in a local hospital.

The capacity to give detailed guidelines on corporate policy has an obvious value, but it is limited if the organisation is, as many are, convinced that it needs to have a more rapid local response to the changing environment. Assuming that it is local managers who best understand local conditions, then they will make the optimum judgement about persons employed, local or expatriates, in their locale. Many organisations have, therefore, decided to adopt a decentralised and relatively informal approach to the terms and conditions under which staff are employed in overseas companies, partnerships, subsidiaries and joint ventures. The value of the role of the international corporate policeman is thus lessened.

The international developer presents another role which the HR professional could adopt. This role is primarily concerned with identifying, both individually and in groups, the training and development needs which are associated with the requirements of a global business. An obvious example would be the need to train expatriates about the specific conditions, customs, and ways of behaving in the culture into which they are relocated. The role would also be concerned with the identification of potential transferees to particular countries or the location of potential general management talent within countries or continents.

Although there is a role for individuals who can provide these general packages of selection and development, it may be that the need is declining, because of the recognition that local staff make effective local HR managers. If this is the case then fewer expatriate managers will be required.

There is a growing understanding of the difficulty of convincing staff, whether or not they have partners, to be mobile for a significant number of years. The growth of dual career families is one of the major factors in this difficulty. Therefore, there may in the future be less likelihood of country or continent general managers who willingly move across continents to take more senior positions. The role of the HR manager in the international environment may be similar to that undertaken in the local environment. He may, in either setting, become a *challenging partner* to line managers rather than an 'expert' power-based director or a provider of a series of global training initiatives. The role of challenging partner may well cover:

- the foundation of local staff development and training
- guidance, not direction, of local management on the utilisation of available financial resources for compensation and benefit
- counselling, as appropriate, teams, inter-team and organisational development
- the provision of personal and third party counselling for expatriate and partner stress.

Expatriate stress

The problems of living abroad may be considered in terms of the reaction of the expatriate to the new culture. The following table suggests typical reactions and their likely effects:

Reaction to culture	Effect on person
Assimilation	Integration into host culture – loss of sense of self
Rejection	Possible conflict with host culture – assertiveness
Vacillation	Confusion – identity conflict
Synthesis	Probable personal growth – inter-group harmony

Each personal reaction will have its effect. Some people have referred to it as 'culture shock'. The problems of making the necessary psychological adaptations, the sense of loss of friends, the possibility of rejection by the host culture, the confusion about identity, the anxiety about how to react to cultural differences, and, perhaps, the feeling that one is unable to cope with the new environment, will all tend to make the individual feel displaced and cause come degree of alienation.

The adjustment process could go through the cycle of: curiosity about the new culture, followed by a growing sense of loss of self and of the familiar, with a possible hostility to, or rejection of, the new, and then perhaps, gradually, a sense of assurance in the new until a greater sense prevails that the differences can lead to an increased level of self-actualisation.

The HR professional may be required as a facilitator/counsellor at any stage in an individual's progress towards achieving a productive harmony with the new situation. To be recognised as a counsellor, one would have to be considered, by the expatriate manager, to possess the psychological aptitude and counselling skills to effectively facilitate the passage of relocatees into the new culture. Those HR professionals who have acted as, and enjoyed the role of, corporate policeman will have to undergo a considerable metamorphosis to acquire the requisite skills and insight.

Selecting international managers

The major role of the empowering HR Manager in respect of
expatriates is probably that of the facilitator of selection, in
which capacity s/he will be able to draw upon the experience of
many other international managers. There are some characteristics that have been frequently found to be associated with
successful international managers. They are:

Cognitive
- openness to new ways of exploring the world
- capacity for assimilating new information rapidly
- ability to analyse new information rapidly
- capacity for remaining open to others' explanation of the
  information
- constant search for new information which could explain the
  situation more effectively
- personal capacity for generating new explanations

Interpersonal
- wide range of communication and persuasion styles
- ability to identify rapidly the most effective style for any
  situation
- openness to feedback
- wide range of team member styles
- search for feedback on effectiveness of planned style

Management
- wide range of management styles
- ability to judge appropriateness of particular style rapidly
- openness to feedback on particular style
- capacity for performing effectively without expert or positional
  power
- ability to manage with little personal guidance

Personal
- enjoyment of cultural diversity

- high adaptability to circumstances
- emotional resilience
- tolerance of alternative and conflicting attitudes, values and ethics
- patience with different cognitive, interpersonal and managerial approaches
- self-sufficiency and resourcefulness
- confidence and independence

Functional (skill and knowledge)
- wider knowledge than own function
- ability to acquire new knowledge and skills rapidly
- familiarity with host country culture, politics and religion
- capacity for operating at tactical and strategic levels

Familial
- resilience and self-sufficiency.

The HR professional can be a 'challenging partner' by ensuring that these characteristics are included and applied in assessments to determine any transfer or promotion decisions which involve international contexts.

The HR manager needs to be sure that the methods used are devoid of cultural bias if they are to be thoroughly effective. Do tests exist which measure the desired characteristics in a manner which the individual will fully comprehend? Are they in the individual's first language? Are there norms against which the individual may realistically be judged?

For example, if a manager in India is to be judged suitable to transfer to work in Canada, are the methods of assessment applied in that manager's first language? Does the test for 'innovative capacity' assess the same qualities as that applied to Canadian or European managers? Are the indicators of performance, in any given assessment, the same as those sought from Canadian managers? Can we accurately assess the personal dynamics of someone who has internalised Indian culture and then compare them with those who have internalised French-Canadian culture? Can we predict the career dynamics of an Indian manager in terms of Anglo-American models of management?

Given the extensive range of questions that can be related to the process of making judgements about people from other cultures in order to be a 'challenging partner', the HR professional needs to have a wide range of skills. They could include

- considerable knowledge of other cultures
- a wide knowledge of assessment methods and their cultural determinants
- and considerable capacity for working together with external third parties who might be used to undertake assessments.

Developing international managers

As a competent developer of international managers, the HR professional would ensure that employees who are to be transferred are sufficiently:

- informed about the host country, or at least that they are aware of the sources of this information
- sensitised to the culture of the host country.

International developers will also create opportunities for staff to learn how best to cope with new cultures, probably by enabling individuals to experience career challenges, such as:

- negotiations in other countries
- dealing with technology changes abroad
- arranging supplier relationships across national boundaries
- managing a small international team through a limited change
- marketing in another culture.

These challenges are usually short but 'real' projects, which should commence in the early years of employment, with 'limited' trials, and which can progress to larger projects, such as, for example, working on a team to convince another country that an environmentally sensitive region should welcome the building of a manufacturing unit.

Compensation and benefits

The 'challenging' international developer has to ensure that having facilitated the selection and preparation of staff, the terms and conditions will motivate and retain them. Assuming that the business is not centralised and formalised, this will be achieved through a process of problem identification and solution, rather than by the provision of the 'one best way'. Again, the HR professional will need to be capable of analysing the available data, whilst also sensing which cultural, organisational and managerial practices and procedures will prove most successful in a given case.

There are a number of organisations which will provide advice on the cost of living in a particular country, and will indicate the salary levels for particular skills in that country, and the range of benefits that can be expected by managers at varying levels. What they will not be able to do is to sense the capacity of an individual, group or organisation to accept and be motivated by a particular compensation and benefit package. The HR professional, on the other hand, should be sufficiently experienced to appreciate the requirements and expectations of relocating managers.

The case study which follows shows how an HR professional, in a relatively formalised and centralised business, was able to facilitate line management objectives of those responsible for establishing a manufacturing plant in the Ukraine.

The study provides examples of how HR can act as a *challenging partner* to line management, when its processes and practices are fully integrated within the corporate strategy. By seeking to empower the line through his actions as advisor and counsellor the HR Director was able to facilitate significant change in a difficult political and economic environment. He concludes that it was a major learning experience for him. It provides rich material for others to learn from.

Case study

An organisational start up in Eastern Europe

As a company, Allied-Lyons already had experience of trading with Eastern Europe and with Russia in particular. Through Baskin-Robbins, the American ice cream company, they had established a joint venture in retail distribution in Moscow, as well as a commitment to build an ice cream plant in that city. Hiram Walker had been supplying hard currency shops with international spirit and liqueur brands for many years; however, if the market was to develop on a market economy basis for the future, the nature of the business would change and early experience was therefore vital.

At this time, Western governments were encouraging their business enterprises to invest and to bring modern technology (especially food technology) and business disciplines to the ailing economies of the Eastern Bloc.

It was against this background that Allied-Lyons, through Hiram Walker, was looking for a business partner within the former Soviet Union. Although the company had experience of working within Eastern Europe, the continuing political, economic and legal uncertainties, together with the required scale of change, made it sensible for Allied-Lyons to be cautious in their approach. This was not the time to risk millions of pounds of shareholders' money.

A key element for the success of any joint venture is the

ability to create hard currency earnings to fund future investment requirements, whilst at the same time generating cash
locally to sustain the day to day operating expenses of the
enterprise. Whilst profit and return on capital are important
measures of business success, the political risk factors were
such that any projections in this area had to be treated with
scepticism.

A partner was found in Agrofirm Prut, which operated five
collective farms and associated industrial units in Kolomiya,
Western Ukraine, some 500 miles south west of Kiev. Prut
had a good water source and was actively involved in
bottling mineral water and soft drinks for the local markets.
It also had an abundant supply of apples and other fruits.
Some tentative steps had been made to produce concentrated
apple juice, though both quality and yield were poor
through lack of technical know-how and outdated plant and
equipment.

The challenge was clear. The concentrating and bottling
activities would be combined into a joint venture, to be run on
western lines. Al-Prut would put into the venture the land,
buildings and plant, whilst Hiram Walker would supply the
technology, training and business expertise. Additionally,
through Allied-Lyons, hard currency loans would be established to enable initial investments to be made. The joint
venture, however, had to be able to stand on its own feet
financially. Financial viability was considered a very important
step in the change process – if you are going to embrace a
market economy, you cannot expect to be bailed out every
time the going gets tough.

A challenge for East and West

The challenge of change was not going to be felt just by those
from the East: the team assigned from Hiram Walker was
going to feel that challenge, too. Kolomiya is, by any stretch
of the imagination, isolated: there are, still, no international

telephone lines; flying from Kiev is fraught with risk, because
of delay and cancellation; by train, the journey takes some 14
hours, and causes you to praise British Rail! The area had
been closed to Westerners since the Russian revolution and,
whilst food is generally always available, choice is not. The
normal forms of business support, which we take for granted,
are unavailable. Isolation is a real problem, and would
at times stretch the team to its limits. Additionally, the
external environment was in a state of lonstant flux. At first,
the joint venture was subject to Soviet law, and Russian was
the primary language; but with Ukrainian independence, there
was a change to Ukrainian law (which was developing and
changing by the day) and Ukrainian became the primary
language.

For the Eastern partners, the challenge was even greater.
They were to be exposed to the full rigours of a market
economy for the first time as they embraced a Western-style
management culture. They had no clear vision what that
meant. A market economy was one which provided nice cars,
radio cassette players, videos, Levi jeans, Ballantine's Scotch
and Nike trainers. As such, they wanted to be part of it.
However, the notion that these items were purchased out of
wealth generation, which system involves risks such as unemployment, was alien to their understanding of economic forces.
Similarly, ideas of quality and hygiene were not well understood in an economy where the state had guaranteed to buy all
production regardless of standards. Principles of Anglo-Saxon
business ethics were a source of future tension.

As the joint venture developed, these factors would challenge both parties.

The vision   There are two fundamental ingredients in successful change management. Without them, managed change
will not happen. First, there must be a clear **vision**, comprising
beliefs and values concerning what the change process is to
deliver: without these beliefs and values, sustainable change is
not possible. Second, those who are to be affected directly by

the change process must show a **willingness to embrace change**. This is normally demonstrated by ostensible dissatisfaction with the current situation coupled with willingness to share the vision of new beliefs and values.

In the early 1990s, there was great expectation of change within the Ukraine, a feeling of eventual liberation. Few people, however, understood what change would really bring and how it would affect them. There was a real danger that they wanted change for change's sake, and were unable to evaluate its effects realistically. It would be vital to keep people's feet on the ground in order to control the change in manageable steps, and so ensure delivery. We were equally convinced of the need for a stretching vision for the enterprise. If we were to be true to the brief of creating an enterprise with Western values, then we would have to embrace best practice in terms of business performance. It was on this basis that we agreed a mission and strategic objectives for our joint venture.

Mission   With international co-operation the joint venture will produce high quality, profitable, bulk and packaged products for export and domestic markets – through the application of modern technololgy and best management practices, utilising a well-trained, motivated and rewarded workforce.

Strategic objective
1. To create a new and progressive business culture by the incorporation of Western management practices.
2. To establish cost effective manufacturing units that achieve Western standards of safety, quality, productivity and flexibility.
3. To develop the production and sale of good quality apple concentrate to generate the joint venture's hard currency requirements.
4. To establish an effective position in the domestic market by

developing the production and sale of good quality bottled drinks and purées.

As we were to move into the detailed planning and set up phases of the operation, this clear and concise mission statement was going to be an important source of reference and help in overcoming the many problems we were going to face on a day-to-day basis. It presented a clear value-set and vision for what we wanted to achieve and became a reference point by which we could check out our decisions: did they help to fulfil the mission? The mission statement also provided a key framework for the development of individual objectives and critical success factors within the operation.

Establishing and managing the Western input

The manner in which we were to provide the Western input and management over time was an important consideration. Given the isolation of the operation, there was concern about the practicability of assigning anyone to the location on a full-time basis. HR had a strong belief, however, which was quickly justified, that, without a full-time Western presence on location in the initial period, the regression factor would be such that we would constantly be catching up from the last visit so that little real progress would be made. There were strong arguments for a three-man team on site covering production, finance and Human Resource management. However, whilst this would have given us the advantage of mutual support, the venture was of insufficient size to sustain such a cost base. In the event, we agreed to appoint – on an international assignment basis – a Western Deputy General Director, with a production/project management bias.

We were fortunate in so far as we were able to appoint from our existing work force Simon Bluck, a young man who was 'looking for a challenge and international experience'! Simon had particular attributes which were important to us: mild-mannered and almost unflappable, he had spent many holidays back-packing in places such as Peru and the Himalayas. These factors were as important as his production and project management skills, and much of the success of the joint venture would be down to him and his partner, Pippa Grayston, who also worked for Hiram Walker.

The terms of their assignment were a key factor which we had to plan. We had to be prepared to take a flexible approach, and this included provision of a role for Pippa, who used the assignment to study for an MBA, as well as providing support to Western input through her purchasing management skills. Few HR professionals can have been responsible for assigning someone to such a remote location, where there is no established ex-pat community. Although the HR Director, Len Sheen, had had experience of the management of people in 'nasty' places, these always involved compound living and contact with other ex-pats. Obviously, regular 'Rest and Recuperation' breaks, communications and the provision of Western-standard housing, were imperative. The financial terms would also need to provide an incentive – but this had to be 'balanced', as the acceptance of the assignment purely for financial gain would have led to disaster. A more important consideration was that such an assignment would lead to longer-term career enhancement for the individuals concerned.

The lack of international telecommunications in the area (apart from unreliable telex links) was a real problem, which had to be overcome – both from a business point of view, and, equally importantly, from a personnel point of view. As a company, we were not prepared to assign employees to an area which was remote *and* potentially politically unstable, without reliable communications. Fortunately, the problem was overcome by the installation of a satellite communications system, although, with call charges costing £6 per minute, this was not a cheap solution!

These factors were essential to the success of our business plan. Whilst it is not always popular to emphasise such practical 'hygiene' factors when considering the change process, today, as we are all constantly directed towards the measurement of the bottom line, we ignore the work of Maslow and Herzberg on motivation at our peril, particularly in situations such as this.

The next important step was to establish the Western Project Team, which would develop and manage the initial phases of the project. We were able to put together a multi-discipline team, which would bring the joint venture to life. Under the overall direction of Tony Allen, our Technical Director and a food technologist by training, the team covered Manufacturing and Technical, Human Resources, Commercial, Finance and Planning, and, importantly, translation functions.

Personnel covering these disciplines were to become regular visitors to Kolomiya during the year September 1991 to September 1992, as we moved from set up to full operation. The timing was important because of the apple harvest and the need to generate hard currency through the production of apple concentrate for the world market. Additionally, weather was a consideration, as snow and temperatures down to minus 30C would make travel difficult between November and February.

In selecting the team, a number of factors were important:

- the need to assign senior managers to the project
- individual abilities and knowledge
- a capacity for working outside of own discipline and sharing the vision
- resourcefulness
- willingness to live and work together in close harmony.
- A sense of humour.

Given the location, the possession of a sense of humour became a very important factor. The team were given the top floor of a farm house as accommodation in which they both worked and lived, in very close quarters, for two or three weeks at a time, with nowhere to go and no contact by phone to home. It is a tribute to the entire team that no one fell out and everyone kept a sense of humour, even when the lights and water failed. None of the team were inexperienced when it came to foreign travel, but top class business hotels do not compare with sharing a room and having a rota for showers, as the system could only produce two hot-to-warm showers at a time. The rota therefore stipulated two in the morning, two at lunch and two at night – but frequent power cuts could disrupt water supplies. A sensible precaution, therefore, was always to fill the basin with water prior to entering the shower – just in case!

This may seem a light hearted factor, though it had a very serious side too. Such factors can cause much friction in a team working together so closely, and have to be considered in team selection. Indeed, the culture of some companies may be such that their executives could not accept such an environment. If that is the case, they should not embark on such a project.

It also became clear that on such a remote project, although senior people were needed in order to provide breadth of vision and, on occasion, the clout to get things done, everyone had to be prepared to muck in and, at times, work on more menial tasks: the team had to be self supporting. Whilst the close quarters and isolation created hardship, they also helped to develop the team, and it was interesting to see the spin-off advantages which came from the exercise in terms of team building, leadership and self-development. These were positive achievements, which should not be underestimated.

Adjoining the local management

Having developed a clear vision, we had to obtain the 'buy in' of our partners and the local management to that set of values and beliefs. Although they could understand and were willing to embrace many of the ideas, they did not then have the necessary detailed knowledge of the workings of a Western enterprise to understand the implications of our values and beliefs. There was a danger that they would buy into concepts which they did not understand and which they would later be forced to disown. The General Director, Company Secretary/ Translator and Engineering Manager had visited our operations in the UK, but they did not at that stage have any real knowledge of our management philosophy or of what this 'Holy Grail' of the market economy meant on a day-to-day basis. We had planned a management training programme for the senior team, although that would not take place until after all the mangement team had been appointed. Before then, much work had to be done.

We decided therefore to move straight into the development of the organisational structure and the sizing of the headcount: this would be used as a mechanism to establish how the venture would operate in practice, what the inter-relationships would be, and who would be accountable for what. This was to prove a difficult and tedious process. Nevertheless, the time we spent in debate, and the patience shown by our team at this stage, was essential to the learning process for both sides. It enabled us to develop a clear vision of how we needed to proceed for the future, as we moved into the more fundamental day-to-day activities of job definition and design.

There were no real equivalents to our notions of delegation and personal accountability in the former Soviet Union. The General Director was the decision maker, and staff were expected to carry out his instructions without question. There was no middle management structure. The results were long lines of people outside of the GD's office awaiting decisions, and other people trying to fulfil his latest request – regardless of whether they were suited to perform the task. Organisational paralysis frequently ensued.

Once we had been successful in communicating our notions of responsibility, delegation and accountability, a major stumbling block was overcome. This was achieved, in part, by explaining how the organisation proposed to work. There were twin benefits: first, we had to prove that we had got it right; and, second, our partners really understood what it was we were trying to achieve. Put like that, our problem of conveying what these notions mean in our business culture would appear to have been surmounted with relative ease.

The truth of the matter was, however, that we were forced into a detailed defence of our proposals, because our partners genuinely had difficulty in understanding what we were trying to achieve. This has a message for all of us involved in the development of organisations and teams: for, how often do we *really explain how* our proposed organisations are going to work? Perhaps, if we spent more time developing to the full our understanding of the implications of the changes we propose, and then had to fully explain how we expected behaviour to change, we would be more successful in achieving sustainable change. As Roger Plant said in his very readable book, *Managing Change and Making It Stick* (Gower, 1987): 'Unless behaviour changes – nothing changes'.

Back to basics

Having achieved a shared vision of the organisation with our partners, we then moved into a detailed planning stage, which involved us in:

- describing and profiling each job within the venture
- developing recruitment and selection procedures
- establishing criteria for remuneration, pay rates and review
- establishing employment contracts and staff handbooks
- developing training needs analyses and programmes.

At the same time, the team were getting to grips with the organisation of production, with commercial and legal arrangements and the development of accounting standards to meet both Ukrainian and UK requirements. All of these aspects had clear implications for the work of the HR professionals. The situation was dynamic and changing, and we had to respond.

No one should underestimate the amount of detail which had to be dealt with during this stage, and much of this work would, in other circumstances, have been delegated to young, and therefore relatively inexperienced, staff. Circumstances had, however, directed me to a different path, and I had brought into the project Brian Goodsell, and experienced UK personnel manager who had decided to take early retirement following the reorganisation of our UK activities. Brian was prepared to tackle the detail of the project, which included writing around 30 job descriptions and specifications covering the 100+ positions in the enterprise. The experience he brought to the process proved to be invaluable. His 'grey hair' also proved a source of comfort to the Ukrainian team. In both respects, we would have lost out had the tasks been delegated to a younger staff member. Brian's experience also helped us all to keep our feet on the ground and ensured that what we proposed was manageable. The experience which an 'old hand' with vision can bring to a project such as this should not be underestimated.

Job descriptions and specifications were also new to our partners, but they were readily embraced, as was the need for flexibility in order to meet change. It had been agreed that the management of the venture would, in the main, be recruited locally, although the general workforce would be recruited from within Prut. Whilst there were advantages to working for a JV, in the form of better wages and conditions, access to Western goods, being at the vanguard of change, etc., the fact was that local personnel would be giving up a job for life in doing so. Fortunately, Prut had agreed that they would absorb those people who were not required by the venture at the start up. But we had to be as certain as we could be that we made the right people choices, as the State had no mechanisms to cope with unemployment as such.

We needed a systematic selection process, but the use of occupational testing was ruled out as competence tests for the Ukraine were unavailable. We therefore had to rely upon interviews plus simple skill tests. At the same time, our partners had no experience of selection interviewing, as in the past they had to accept the workers assigned to them. We therefore needed to establish a simple but effective system to help guide them in the process, a system which our own team could work with as well. We looked at the National Institute of Industrial Psychology's Seven Point Plan and at John Munro Fraser's adaptation of it into his Five Fold Grading System. In the end, we used a simplified format of the Munro Fraser system, which worked well and was readily understood by our partners. Many may feel that we have developed beyond Munro Fraser, but its success in this situation perhaps says two things: first, the Ukrainian state of development would not lend itself to more complex models at this time; and second, adopting a structured interviewing technique may be of assistance to many managers.

All employees were taken on an initial 3-month trial period, and then on 12-month fixed term contracts – there being no provision for dismissal, other than for gross misconduct, in Ukrainian labour law. At the end of the first 12 months of operation, all employees were assessed and appraised on the basis of job performance, time keeping and attendance, and attitude/team contribution. As a result, of the original 100+ employees selected, 95% were adjudged effective and retained; 2% had left of their own volition, and 3% did not have their contracts renewed. This was a remarkably good result, which is attributable to a number of factors:

- good management
- good performance by the production units
- above average terms and conditions
- effective induction and job training
- a culture which encourages team work
- the enthusiasm of both the General Director and his Deputy to succeed.

The development of terms and conditions was not altogether straightforward. We were able to draw on the experience of other companies, in a process which it is fashionable to call 'benchmarking'. The experience of our colleagues in Baskin-

Robbins, together with experience from McDonalds and Tam Brands, were helpful in the development of our own terms and conditions and our staff handbook. What we were to develop, however, had to be right for *our* operation and had to meet *our* own beliefs and values.

We had to debate the question of the right to lay off workers without pay. A major concern was the availability of materials for the bottling line, because bottle supplies could often dry up. If we could not run the line, should we have the right to send workers home without pay? We wanted to adopt best practice in terms of resourcing, and that said that management had the responsibility to ensure supplies – there should be no easy let out. In the end, we went back to our mission and shared values: lay off in those circumstances was not acceptable.

We recognised early on in the process that our partners were inexperienced in communicating with their workforce which, as such, had little knowledge of what was going on. We therefore developed for them a communication process, consisting of regular bulletins for the whole workforce and cascade briefings for those directly involved in what was to become the Al-Prut venture. The communication process was to become a central vehicle for achieving success through the promotion of our core values and beliefs.

We did not always get it right. In recruiting the management team, we needed to go outside of Prut. We placed advertisements in local papers, but received a very low response. It was only then that we realised that there had been no communication with the press by our partners, and therefore no press coverage of our venture. A hasty press release was drafted – the first press release ever received by the local papers, who produced it verbatim.

As well as the successful retention of people, the joint venture has achieved its objectives – in terms of both efficiency and quality of production – since its inception. There *have* been problems, but these have resulted from hyperinflation or political risk factors which are difficult to control. Through changes in Ukrainian law, the venture has become a joint stock company which will fulfil its financial commitments to the parties concerned.

For Hiram Walker, it has proved a most useful learning process. The systems and procedures developed for Al-Prut have provided the framwork for the development of successful ventures in Slovenia and in the People's Republic of China. For all of the individuals concerned, the venture has been an important chapter of personal development.

What are the key lessons?

- develop a clear **vision**: shared *beliefs* and *values* are essential
- manageable success is more important than large scale failure
- readiness to accept change is a prerequisite
- careful selection of the team is vital
- basic 'hygiene' factors cannot be ignored
- time spent developing the organisation and how it will work is time well spent
- communicate, communicate and communicate again
- back to basics with job descriptions, person specifications and selection technologies
- use your *values* and *beliefs* in the decision making process
- in any joint venture, choose a compatible partner.

7

Achieving Market Leadership – A Case Study

Marketing has become one of the main forms of business. Its influence has grown rapidly during the past two decades. It is what the Institute of Marketing defines as 'the management process responsible for identifying, anticipating and satisfying customer requirements profitably'. The activities which it covers include: the planning and development of products; the distribution of the products; the establishment of prices and the promotion of the product. Given that the essential principles of marketing include attention to customer needs and wants, satisfaction of those needs and wants at a profit, and orientation of the whole organisation to customer-satisfaction, it would seem that any service for this function should be of prime importance.

To what extent should the Human Resource function be regarded as a service from which Marketing seeks advice and guidance? In many organisations, the HR function provides the 'expert' advice. It gives guidance on where there is a well-defined system, about salaries and benefits. It provides advice on disciplinary and grievance procedures, and gives an occasional welfare/counselling service.

In some organisations, however, the HR function has a merely peripheral role during the recruitment process. The HR professional may become involved as an administrative centre, a post-box for replies to advertisements. S/he may write the letters confirming interviews or draft the formal contracts of employment. In such organisations, HR may not become directly involved in the selection procedure, perhaps because Marketing regards HR professionals as providing a service which lacks sufficient understanding of the function to be able to contribute meaningfully to decisions about the fit of the individual to a job, role, team or organisation.

Again, Marketing may consider that the contribution of HR to training and development consists in the booking of courses. HR is here perceived to act in a way similar to an airline booking office: HR knows the destinations, timings and costs, but cannot advise the customer on the most appropriate choice. The role of the advisor during the process of making decisions about individual, team and/or function development may be performed internally, thus excluding HR, who may book the course, but under the direction of Marketing.

Marketing directors, like the directors of other functions, will require occasional guidance and advice on their department's climate, personal style and their influence. They may ask for advice on the way their teams operate and interact. They may seek guidance on the way their department interfaces with other departments. Or they may ask for help in the consideration of their own development and their career. If HR is perceived as a source of effective facilitation, these questions may be addressed to the function. The case study which follows illustrates how such a negative perception of the HR function can be transformed into an appreciation of HR as an effective advisor to the Marketing function.

Case study: Reckitt & Colman Products

The company is part of Reckitt & Colman PLC, which employs around 22,000 staff. The company manufactures, on a world-wide basis, household, toiletry, food, pharmaceutical and industrial goods.

Reckitt & Colman Products manufactures, markets and sells personal care, pharmaceutical and household products. It employs around 1,000 staff, with bases in Hull, Humberside and Derby. Its products are marketed throughout the world.

The company has a Human Resource function which consists of a director, Personnel Services manager, Training and Development manager, Industrial Relations manager and

Health and Safety manager. Historically, the HR function has been seen as primarily a custodian of HR practice, as the company policeman. A major focus of the role was that of controller and monitor, ensuring that the management and staff followed procedures and practices. Line management have tended to exclude HR from their considerations of major staff and organisational decisions.

A new HR director was appointed about three years ago. He was an ex-Marketing manager, which gave him certain advantages, in particular – credibility as a line manager. He had 'actually managed things', had 'really launched products', 'negotiated prices with suppliers', 'developed ideas', etc. Other line managers therefore considered they could discuss 'real management issues' with him. He could 'understand' cost control, quality initiatives, product segmentation, advertising effectiveness, supplier agreements, etc. Managers came to talk to him because he was considered able to understand their problems.

Amidst this positive climate, the HR director was able to consider emerging business issues and the added value role from his function. As such, he was beginning to assume the 'strategic partner' role. The company at the time had just concluded a major strategic review of its world-wide business operations. Their conclusions were that:

- The business should be organised and run on a world-wide basis with identified strategic product category portfolios, for example in pharmaceutical products, becoming the focus for their strategic thinking
- A major strategic investment was needed in NPD to extend product brands and values
- The manufacturing resource was to be rationalised into focused factories which would supply the world-wide marketing organisation.

These conclusions persuaded the HR Director that his team's strategic contribution would be in supporting the overall change process, reviewing the qualities of the current management and staff against the new role demands, and upgrading the effectiveness and focus of the overall management development strategy. The vehicle he settled on was the introduction of managerial competency-based thinking. The link between defining 'high performance competences' and measuring and developing the current stock of talent attracted both him and his directorial colleagues. We were chosen as the consultancy to support them. In what follows, the approach used is explained and illustrated.

The marketing competency study

Defining the organisational strategy

Reckitt & Colman Products' directors agreed to be inter-viewed. The interviews, of the Finance, Sales, Marketing (2), Development (2), Human Resources and Production directors enabled the company to refine further its goals and critical success factors. It also enabled the company to define more precisely the strategies which would add value and make the biggest difference to corporate success.

Defining the future enabled the company to identify the job elements that would make the greatest impact on profitability. Through a process of interviews with each of the directors, and with a significant sample of those who reported to them, the company identified the critical jobs and their important dimen-sions that would enable it to achieve its objectives.

The HR director was of critical importance to this process. He was able to convince the Board of the crucial value of people in achieving the objective. He was able to explain to his colleagues and the MD the value of a competency study, because he had personally undertaken, as had some of his staff, training in the competency approach. He was further able to ensure that Board colleagues co-operated in a relatively time-consuming project.

Having identified the relevant changes in the business and the ways in which they could influence the required personal characteristics, the project proceeded with a series of Behavioural Event interviews (BEIs).

The BEI's were conducted with critical job holders (those whose jobs would add significant value to the business). In the Marketing function, which covered two product categories – household and pharmaceutical – over 20 interviews were conducted. These interviews, when analyzed through a process of content analysis, coding and then expert panel validation, produced a competency model for particular jobs. The jobs for which models were produced were Marketing manager, Category manager and Brand manager. The analysis also generated a generic competency model for management. This was important, as it could be, and was, used by the HR director as a reason why the processes of succession planning and management development should be company wide, as well as functionally deep.

The final models for the Marketing department were agreed by the whole Board. The HR director was able to persuade the MD and his Board colleagues that he should have a day for a feedback to an expert panel. The result was that the Board developed an understanding of the process and of the potential results, and were therefore enabled to support and act as communicators for the process. They were also more supportive of the further development of the process, which was to undertake Development Centres.

Competency development centres

After identifying the personal qualities that would be required for the future success of the business, there were two major decisions to be made. How would this affect the current staff and how would it influence selection? The initial impact was on current staff.

The HR director determined that the majority of current

staff would be likely to remain, but that with relatively low labour turnover, there was a major need to improve their performance. To achieve this, he instituted the process of development centres. Each development centre would be a two-day event.

The events were to have as their objectives the identification, for the individual assessees, of the quality that they determined would enhance their performance if developed. The events would also help the organisation to identify common development needs and would develop their understanding of individuals' capacities for transfer and growth. Development centres were further expected to help identify those management styles and organisational climate issues which may have been either blocks to or enhancers of performance.

The development centres were held off site, in a hotel. Each had at least two external assessors, and were normally attended by 10 to 12 in-company assessees. The programme consisted of:

- a pre-centre workbook, which was designed to enable individuals to explore their previous, current and future career/life
- the centre itself, which offered a combination of (a) psychometric and projective measures, designed to enable individuals to exhibit their personally preferred behaviours, (b) a number of management simulations, and (c) a career interview.

The HR director's tasks, meanwhile, were to ensure (i) that line management was convinced of the utility of this process; (ii) that the costs were budgeted for; (iii) that the assessees had the time available to attend the centre; and (iv) that, most importantly, the directors of other functions supported by their words and actions the objectives of personal growth and development both pre- and post-centre.

Following each event, individuals – provided with both

verbal and written feedback reports – were actively engaged in writing their own career development reviews. Again, the HR director had to ensure that assessees had the time (1–2 hours) available.

Unusually, they had the opportunity to edit their reports so that they best represented their understanding of themselves. Often this needed a number of feedback meetings.

The HR Director's had to ensure that his colleagues accepted that self-motivated assessment and learning were effective, and also that time was made available for the meetings necessary to producing the final report, which went to the company.

Marketing directors, in both Household and Pharmaceutical Divisions, ensured that the majority of their staff went to these Centres. Their role was seen to be central to the market-driven strategy. The outputs were used by the HR director and his staff to counsel the Marketing directors and their staff on personal development needs, common training needs, managerial style and how it influenced performance, functional climate and how it enhanced or inhibited performance. Specifically, the HR director was a major focus for the development of common programmes, designed to improve the performance of staff capacity to:

- influence without positional or expert power
- think more critically about information
- and for senior management, act as a coach and a developer.

The programme of development centres also highlighted the need for an increased capacity to manage cross-functionally. This led to an organisational development effort designed to increase the effectiveness of the relationships between Marketing and Sales, and Marketing and Development.

The HR director had moved his function from the traditional position of controller of the rules to that of facilitator of improved performance. He would rarely be heard quoting the procedures, but was observed actively listening to business profit-orientated problems and then seeking to identify which personal, interpersonal or organisational initiatives were needed in order that organisation goals could be achieved.

Competency selection systems

Although it was recognised that the majority of staff would remain and, therefore, that a significant effort should be made to increase current staff performance, it was also recognised, particularly in Marketing that new staff would need to be recruited to meet future demands. The HR director therefore convinced his colleagues that all new managerial, or potential managerial, staff should be assessed against the defined success-related competencies.

This meant that he and his staff had to ensure:

- that all job descriptions became competency-based
- that all search and/or selection consultancies had to be briefed in terms of competency, and their performance evaluated against the new success criteria
- that all application forms were redesigned to allow competency-based judgements to be made
- that the interviewing process be redesigned so that individuals were assessed, during interview, against the competency success criteria
- that interviewers were able to conduct competency-based interviews.

The HR Director had thus to convince his colleagues and the MD that the time and expense invested in the new phase of the programme would produce the desired results. The new approach to the graduate recruitment programme included:

- a biodata-weighted application form
- a competency-based interview process, conducted by line and HR staff,

- a competency-based assessment centre, which was a one-day process for shortlisted candidates
- feedback for both successful and unsuccessful candidates.

These measures were designed to ensure that selected individuals fitted into the new organisation, as well as possible, and that the company's profile amongst potential employees – students – was as high as possible.

Competency-based appraisal processes

The company's appraisal procedure was generally goal, rather than process, oriented. It emphasised what *should* be achieved rather than *how* and *with which* competencies. The establishment of a generic competency profile as well as functional profiles meant that the company could concentrate part of the appraisal process on a discussion of the degree to which an individual possessed the required competencies and, where there were deficiencies, which procedure would be best suited to develop them.

The HR director and his staff ran a series of seminars designed to develop all managerial staff's understanding of

- the competency terminology
- the appraisal documentation
- the process of appraisal interviewing for competency.

The HR director, recognising the degree of commonality amongst the identified development needs, instigated a programme of development activities designed to improve overall performance.

Competency development programmes

The discussions between the HR director and the Marketing directors identified a number of common development needs, among them:

- increased width of business knowledge and skills
- the capacity to think through issues and problems critically
- the ability to influence and persuade outside areas of personal expertise
- teamwork, both within Marketing and between Marketing and other functions.

Individual development needs were met on a personal basis. The common needs were met by a project-type process and, where necessary, by individual skill or knowledge enhancement. The Marketing directors and their senior managers were helped to increase their coaching skills so that they could become more successful developers.

The pharmaceutical example

Reckitt & Colman had decided to move from drug discovery to semi-ethical OTCs products. They were already the UK's no 1 OTC company in sales value.

The Marketing director had determined that he wanted to establish a culture of endemic change, rather than the existing culture, which emphasised the attitude of 'What is in it for me?', tending to restrict change orientation and perhaps increasing resistance to change. He needed to involve his staff in the change process. The competency project was one of the ways in which he could achieve it.

The definition of top jobs in terms of competency encourages the individual to consider the role and the qualities needed for success. It encourages people to think more strategically, less tactically. It gives one avenue for top management to discuss with other staff why they need to change their behaviour if they wish to succeed and achieve their career potential. Furthermore, when other jobs and replacements were being considered, it provided an opportunity to discuss the changing competency needs for success. The development of the language of competency enabled all managers to move towards a common framework for discussing people and jobs.

The Marketing director recognised, as did the Pharmaceutical Development Director, that too many unsuccessful projects had progressed too far, and perhaps that too many potentially successful projects had been killed too early. Both also recognised that to satisfy global as well as local marketing needs, they would have to change not only their strategy, but also how individuals responded to the challenge of change.

The involvement of the HR director, with his previous Marketing background, was crucial. It ensured that there was a uniformity of approach across the company, and that where there were common needs, they were met. It helped ensure that the standards for promotion and selection were undertaken in a relatively common manner, namely, against competency profiles. Where there were organisational development needs, particularly on joint projects, such as new product development, he provided the guidance, counsel and facilitation so that the combined talents of Development and Marketing were brought to focus on important projects or problems.

The process of market leadership based on identifying potential new products, developing them at the optimum speed, ensuring that they are marketed in the right package and to the correct people at the right time in the best way and at the optimum price, was enhanced by HR defining the qualities required and advising on the selection of people who possessed them. HR was also instrumental in developing internal staff's capacity to exhibit the requisite qualities, encouraging senior staff to coach them; and in facilitating staff's capacity, in groups or one to one, to encourage each other's performance.

Lessons on achieving market leadership

To achieve market leadership, companies should ask themselves:

- Have we fully visioned our future?
- Do we properly understand the qualities of the people who can enhance our vision?
- Do we have procedures designed to ensure that we select and develop the required competencies?
- Is our management able to coach our required competencies?
- Does our current structure and organisation enhance or inhibit the performance of these competencies?
- Does our HR Director and team have the confidence of the line management?
  - Are they fully involved in all business decisions?
  - Are they decision makers or implementers?
  - Does their influence extend to all functions, and is it equally strong at all levels?
- Are the processes of selection, development, appraisal and team development fully integrated with the strategic plan?
- Do all managers use a common language to describe and evaluate other staff?
- Do Marketing and Development managers/directors frequently seek the counsel of the HR director/managers for other than organisational compliance issues?

8

▓ Integrating Mergers and Acquisitions – A Case Study

Mergers and acquisitions are daily news in today's financial world. They produce great press drama, and are normally accompanied by significant expectations of change. They are expected to produce more successful organisations than those which preceded them as independent, unmerged companies.

Reasons for failed mergers/acquisitions

A number of studies have shown that the failure rate of mergers and acquisitions is significantly high. In a study by McKinsey, over two thirds of the acquisitions examined generated less profit, as a percentage, than would have been earned had the money spent on acquisition been deposited in a clearing bank. Another study, by Coopers and Lybrand, has shown that of the 40 companies reviewed, none had achieved its pre-merger stated objectives. Although there is some debate over the methods used to measure precise degrees of success or failure, it is reasonable to suggest that the actual benefits of mergers and acquisitions have generally fallen short of expectations.

Although a number of different explanations may be given to account for these failures, it would seem that a common underlying – and perhaps critical – factor is a failure to deal adequately with the people dimension throughout the merger and acquisition process.

Pre-merger/acquisition research

The research conducted prior to targeted mergers and acquisitions is obviously important, and usually consists of a detailed, systematic analysis of the relevant financial and commercial aspects. The analysis of finances will usually be carried out by an accounting department, while taxation specialists will assess the tax implications of takeover or merger. Legal specialists will examine articles of association, contracts and legal agreements; marketing and sales departments may well be required to consider sector relationships. Property specialists, too, could be involved in the appraisal of non-financial assets.

It is, however, rare for HR departments to be involved in these pre-merger/takeover investigations: it is assumed, apparently, that the 'due diligence', which has to be shown for legal and financial analyses, need not be applied to staff. HR departments tend to become involved only when the company has announced its intention to acquire another, and has pursued that acquisition to the point of an agreement. It is at this stage that the acquisitor's management will *have* to recognise any personnel issues affecting the venture's success.

HR departments, particularly those with specialists or which choose to use specialist external consultants, are probably in a strong position to advise organisations on the best ways of meeting the people challenge of mergers and takeovers. When a HR department is consulted at an earlier stage in the acquisition or merger process, there is a greater likelihood of identifying and meeting such important personnel challenges, and therefore of significantly affecting the success of that process.

The recent failed merger of the **Leeds Permanent Building Society** and the **National & Provincial Building Society** may give some indication of the importance of a HR pre-acquisition investigation.

Case study: Incongruous management styles

Judging from personal communication and news comment, the merger was progressing in terms of the research investigation into the relevant financial, information technology, property and legal aspects. The respective HR departments, however, recognised certain issues which might well be very difficult to overcome.

The pre-merger opportunities for the HR departments of the Leeds and National & Provincial to meet and discuss appear to have given rise to speculation about a possible clash of cultures. The Leeds, with its more formal, centralised and hierarchical organisation, and the National & Provincial, with its competency-based, process orientated culture each had a HR department well-suited to their respective cultures.

The Leeds HR department was characterised by hard processes and practices which corresponded with the rather bureaucratic culture of the organisation (exemplified by their adherence to the Hay Salary System).

The National & Provincial, in contrast, had a change agent orientated HR function, which is indicative of how their processes supported a more fluid structure. For example, the Leeds' HR staff seemed to act as 'experts', while National & Provincial's HR staff sought to be 'facilitators'. The Leeds had a 'traditional' management style, whereas National & Provincial's style was closer to matrix management. It may well be that the recognition of unresolved differences such as these was among the critical factors which resulted in the decision to end the merger process.

The joint search by the HR departments for agreement on systems, procedures and practices made the differences between their styles and methods apparent. Among the lessons to be learned from this unsuccessful venture are that:

- organisations should be clearer about their current and intended cultures prior to any merger initiatives
- the profile of the HR departments of companies involved in mergers should be significantly raised, and their participation in discussions brought forward in the process.

A suggested role for HR in pre-merger research

It may be instructive to consider what typically happens in the pre-acquisition phase, so that opportunities for HR involvement may be identified and highlighted.

The initial phase may be described as exploratory. The managements of the two companies which have identified that an acquisition or merger would be in the interests of both have an opportunity to explore the terms of their projected relationship. It could be at this point that the respective HR departments are used as facilitators of the relationship building process. As the exploration continues, the HR departments may be in a position to gain representation on the evaluation team, which is charged with responsibility for assessing the data relating to the takeover/merger.

HR's role within this should be to evaluate the strength of the senior management team. Very rarely, however, are HR persons allowed access at this stage to the takeover target's team. If it was a friendly takeover, then there would undoubtedly be significant time spent with the senior management team in meetings. The majority of this time, however, would be taken up by discussions on financial, legal and marketing data. It would be unusual for any more thorough assessment than an impressionistic one to be made of a senior management team in the course of such meetings.

Assessing 'targeted' senior management

Because the quality and management philosophy of the human resource at a senior level is of such importance, it would seem to be imperative that the organisation to be acquired has its senior decision makers systematically assessed.

To ensure that individuals are assessed against a clearly defined culture, HR departments need to ensure that they have fully explored, with their Boards, their organisational values. The HR department should undertake a corporate assessment.

In *Corporate Assessment*, A. Furnham and B. Gunter (Routledge, 1993) propose that such an assessment would involve:

- identifying the culture of the acquiring company
- deciding on any changes which would ensure that that culture supports the corporate strategy
- identifying potential acquisitions and their cultures
- isolating likely changes to those cultures
- designing a format for assessing other cultures
- establishing criteria by which to decide in favour of targetted mergers/acquisitions.

Accountants will have access to a considerable body of financial data to which they will apply their professional judgement, giving the decision makers objective advice on cash flow, taxation position, etc. Some HR information is likely to be available on the career backgrounds and skills of senior HR personnel in the target company, although this is not always the case.

Therefore, at the minimum, the HR department should ensure that at this discussion stage they have access to detailed personal, career, educational and other biographical information about each member of the Holding Company's board, plus some information on the boards of subsidiary companies. This information should be used to judge the suitability of those individuals for positions within a merged organisation. This assumes, however, that the HR department has been consulted on the structure of the newly acquired merged company, and has developed from this structure descriptions of the jobs that would be available in the new organisation together with person specifications for each position.

HR will already have detailed biographical information relating to senior personnel within the acquiring company, and will, therefore, be in a position to carry out an initial job/person matching exercise. This will enable the acquiring company to become aware of any gaps. Such gaps would appear where neither the acquired nor the acquiring company had current personnel with the characteristics needed to perform specific defined jobs; or where the personnel available to fill these jobs were limited in terms of skill, knowledge or previous experience; or, perhaps, where potential conflicts between the acquired and acquiring organisations are identified – for example, if personnel from each company are equally qualified to perform the role of a single position.

This limited job/person matching exercise will not, however, provide the same level of objective and detailed analysis that will result from the work of financial or legal analysts. What should be aimed for, nevertheless, is a reliable set of personal analyses – and this will necessitate an in-depth study of the characteristics and abilities of all the senior personnel concerned.

An illustrative scenario

A financial organization which is considering expansion through merger/acquisition had determined that a major HR initiative is required in the development of the acquisition team, and that, in particular, people judgement skills will need to be refined. At this stage, no candidate for acquisition has been identified.

Although a member of the acquisition team the HR department has recognised that, once a candidate has been identified and the process of acquisition initiated, the pace of the process and the concentration of effort will reduce the likelihood of a major HR initiative on the systematic assessment of senior personnel. The department considers it likely that the main contacts between its company and the target company will be conducted by business analysts, accountants, lawyers and 'outside' experts in merchant banking. The HR Director has therefore decided that in the circumstances, the most important initiative that can be undertaken, pre-acquisition, is the development of the acquisition team's skills in assessing people. In this way, the HR department can make a significant contribution to the acquisition process, by enhancing the skills of the accountants, lawyers and line managers involved in assessing the abilities and qualities of the target company's senior management.

A number of questions about the target's management will require clear answers, including:

- how well will they fit with the acquisitor's culture and management style?
- will they meet the acquisitor's requirement in respect of their ability to provide a vision of the future?
- are they sufficiently innovative?
- do they possess the persuasive powers necessary to manage their own staff through change?
- do individual managers have a self-directed and achievement orientated style?

HR, it is agreed, is therefore to provide a development programme designed to improve the skills of their company's acquisition team. They will aim to improve the abilities of team members to gather reliable data about people and to make more verifiable judgements about that data.

During the process of an acquisition, particularly if of the friendly type, it is likely that there will be a negotiation stage, at which both sides are seeking to make a deal. At this stage, the target organisation is unlikely to be willing to allow its senior management to be subject to detailed personal analysis. It is, however, important that good relations between the senior management teams are maintained throughout the negotiations, so that when a deal is struck, there is a willingness to be open.

In general, good relations are readily maintained where the negotiations are conducted by those professional agencies normally used, that is, by merchant banks, commercial lawyers, etc. Following an initial agreement to do a deal, there tends to be a stage at which there is a need for due diligence.

Matching people to jobs

At the stage referred to, the target company is normally subject to considerable further analysis. So it is at this stage that one would expect the HR department to become more directly involved, by following up its initial analysis of the strengths and limitations of the acquired company. This would involve subjecting the target company's top management to systematic analysis.

For many organisations, this would require the use of an external consultancy. In the same way that such consultancies are called in to analyse financial, technical, property and legal situations, so organisations will frequently use external occupational psychologists to analyse the strengths and limitations of the top management of the target company. The provision of a detailed, accurate picture of each member of management of the target company will enable the acquistor to ensure that the matching of jobs to persons is as pragmatic and sensible as is possible. It will further help the acquisitor to ensure that any team which is forged by the merging of two companies' departments bears as few of the scars of conflicted interest as is possible.

This analysis will also reveal details of the differences between the culture of the target and acquiring organisations, such that, where the differences are significant, they can be brought to the attention of the acquiring company's top management. Fundamental differences between the two cultures could be considered a sufficient reason why the acquisition should not go ahead. Where the difference is less than fundamental, top management's planning will cater for it by ensuring that the mission statement's values are communicated to all employees of both companies. Training processes, if necessary, can be used to bring about the desired congruence of values.

The detailed analysis of top management strengths and limitations can be used as the basis for a detailed plan of who should take which position within the newly acquired or merged company. Training solutions to individual skill or aptitude deficiencies can be designed and implemented. Plans for the future, assuming that the company intends to continue to grow, organically or through further acquisition, can be drawn up, so that those with potential for promotion may be developed to achieve the skills and knowledge necessary. The merger of cultures can be planned for and achieved. Thus, in terms of workforce planning as a match to corporate planning, this process is likely to be successful.

Once the task of matching personnel to positions in the merged company is completed, it may be that there is a shortfall on the personnel side, and the process of searching for external candidates to fill such positions should be undertaken as early as possible. It is commonly recognised that it can take six months to a year to acquire 'top' managers. Recruitment procedures should therefore be instituted as soon as any significant gaps in the match are identified. A delay in initiating the recruitment procedure may well result in the newly merged organisation having holes in its workforce which might unnecessarily diminish the effectiveness of the launch of the newly structured organisation.

Matching personnel procedures

The HR department should also keep a watchful eye open for any problems which may arise from the merger of processes and practices of two personnel departments. Problems may stem from variations which exist between the two companies' pension schemes, salary administration systems, terms and benefits applied to various levels of management and staff, and their respective union recognition bargaining situations. Brief comments on the first three areas of potential difference might usefully be made, here.

Pension schemes could provide both an opportunity and a potential problem. They provide an opportunity in the sense that there may be surplus pension funds available, after an acquisition, which could be used as an asset by the merged organisation. There could also be a problem with pension funds, if there are substantial differences between the two companies in terms of the funding rates, the age distribution of their respective benefit differences, the methods of agreement of how benefits should be developed; and the pensions boards of the two companies might be differently constituted.

Salary systems could be a problem if there are real differences between the job evaluation systems. There may well be significant differences between the numbers of grades or the numbers of steps within a particular grade; between the methods for defining jobs and the ways of measuring the differences between the sizes of jobs; between the ways that the salary bands are related to the market, or between the constitutions of job evaluation panels, particularly in terms of union involvement. These variants could well result in conflict between personnel and the organisation if changes are made. Careful scrutiny should therefore be given to existing differences prior to merger or acquisition.

Benefit systems operate differently from company to company, so careful consideration is needed here, too. The acquired organisation may differ fundamentally from the acquisitor in terms of the provision of cars, insurance, life insurance, medical benefits, holiday arrangements, payment of various fees, and the like. If any of these benefits were changed to the detriment of employees of either company, conflict could well ensue.

Therefore, the HR department should be centrally involved in the due diligence stage, examining all factors relating to the fit between personnel systems in the acquired and acquiring organisations, and bringing to the attention of top management any differences or potential causes of conflict, suggesting methods for overcoming these problems. If the conflicts seem to be detrimental to the likely success of the merger or acquisition programme, the HR department should recommend to top management that the programme should not go ahead, at least until agreements are secured to ensure their future resolution.

Evaluating the IR position

Mergers and acquisitions can prove to be fundamentally flawed when due diligence has not been paid to the Trades Union response to being acquired by or merging with a new organis- ation. It has become common in the UK, over the last 10 years, for management to assume the acquiescence of the unions, which, in general, have been less confrontational than used to be the case. It is, therefore, likely to be assumed by manage- ment that the unions will make some initial comment about security of employment, and thereafter fit in with the changes. This assumption is unwarranted. Unions are aware that mergers and acquisitions tend to lead to job losses rather than gains. They are aware that there may follow some fundamental changes to the way in which they are managed. It is likely that they would be aware, too, of the scale of the proposed rationalisation and of changes in job size, job systems and factory methods, etc. They will know that union recognition and bargaining rights are always threatened by management takeovers. It would seem that to assume that a merger or acquisition can progress without any need to consider union reaction is simplistic.

Assuming that the due diligence stage does not result in indications that the process towards merger or acquisition should be halted, there will normally follow a detailed agree- ment on the matters related to the merger or acquisition, and a subsequent approval process. In some cases, the Monopolies and Mergers Commission would be involved. The approval process issues in a completion of the merger or acquisition.

Managing communications

During this whole process, which could last for several months, HR departments should be significantly involved in helping management decide what to communicate to whom, and how that communication could best be managed, so that the relationship between the acquired and acquiring companies or merged organisations remain as friendly as possible; and ensuring that any messages relating to the corporate mission, the reorganising structures, the fitting of people to jobs, and any potential changes to the ways in which people are rewarded or located, may be so transmitted as to maximise motivation to make the merger or acquisition a success, and to minimise the likelihood of conflict.

Without the effective and sympathetic management of this communication, particularly as mergers and acquisitions tend to make good press, it is possible that employees within either the acquiring or acquired organisation could become demotivated, which would have an undesirable effect on performance. It could also affect recruitment – people may not be attracted to organisations in which there is a high level of uncertainty and low motivation, or if press comment suggests potential conflict. Equally, marketable people – who might make the difference between success and failure in the acquisition – could well be subject to headhunting. Unless such individuals feel that there is a significant future for them in the new organisation, they may be tempted to succumb, thereby lessening the chance of success. The HR department, in light of these considerations, could be a significant player in maintaining motivation, developing values and ensuring that communication provides a positive image of the changed organisational state.

The role of HR following merger/aquisition

When the acquisition or merger is formally completed, the HR department could continue to play a major part. Unfortunately, since many organisations will not have involved HR up to this point, the first time that the HR department becomes aware of all the issues relating to the human resource situation in the newly merged or acquired organisation is precisely after the process is complete. The result is often that HR departments feel forced to take a reactive rather than proactive stance, which diminishes their capacities for overcoming problems which should have been recognised and managed with HR involvement at a much earlier stage.

If HR departments have had opportunities of working with top management throughout the acquisition process, there is a greater likelihood that they will perform effective roles toward successful acquisitions or mergers. HR involvement could, for example, help to ensure that:

- the culture of the new organisation supports the business plan
- there is an organisation development programme in position to provide the requisite support
- stress factors are recognised and effective change management measures instituted
- reward systems are in position and that they are supportive of the required performance
- the management style of the two organisations has been analysed and unified in support of the business plan
- the process of fitting people to the new organisation's jobs is effectively managed, and that development programmes are in place to ensure that team members are supportive both of each other and of their team objectives
- there are, where necessary, effective outplacement management initiatives to ensure that personnel who remain are motivated and that those who leave will provide good public relations for the organisation.

Acquisitions and mergers fail most often because of human factors. An unsuccessful takeover is rarely due to failure in the financial, property, legal or other aspects. It is only when HR departments are involved in the whole process of acquisition and merger – that is, from the point at which the target has been identified to the implementation of the merger or takeover – will the level of failure be lowered. The cost of neglecting to involve HR functions must be immense. Ensuring that people perform to the level required to produce the benefits of organisational change – both during and after any merger or acquisition – is a complex process. This discussion contends that the complexity of the process is best reduced through the use of HR professionals and their consultants. When organisations begin to use their HR departments as they use their finance, marketing, legal and property departments, that is by

- recognising their professional expertise, and involving them from the inception of the acquisition/merger process
- allowing them to use such outside specialist consultancies as are considered necessary

then the human resource factor in acquisitions and mergers will provide positive benefits, rather than continuing to be the factor most commonly associated with unsuccessful takeover ventures.

Checklist for the Human Resource department in mergers/acquisitions

- Have you a clear definition of your existing corporate culture? If not, how will you go about generating one?
- Does your culture support your current corporate objectives, and will it support your future merger-acquired objectives? If not, how will you change it?
- Does your acquisition team possess the requisite people judgement skills? How would you improve them?
- Do you have a pre-acquisition/merger plan which provides for the integral involvement of the HR department?
- Are your HR staff knowledgeable about acquisition and merger processes? Would they be capable of making a more influential contribution if they acquired specific knowl-

edge of other relevant specialisms, like finance, banking and law?

- Does your acquisition/merger team, including the HR representatives, have the requisite teamwork skills? How, if necessary, would you enhance them?
- Have you identified and briefed any outside experts who would be called in to your HR staff in making judgements on salaries, benefits, people, structure, processes, practices, culture?
- Have the HR team and its advisors met with and developed their inter-team work objectives and processes with all the internal and external acquisitions staff and advisors, for example, merchant banks, lawyers, accountants, etc? If not, how would you go about the task of bringing all parties together?

The following case study provides an opportunity to explore the degree to which the merger between Zurich and Municipal Mutual met the criteria set out in the checklist. It also gives some insight into how Human Resources acted in a specific merger situation.

Case study: The creation of a new company

As a niche player in the insurance industry, Municipal Mutual Insurance had few equals. Even in its death throes it continued to carry the insurance for some 80 per cent of local authorities. But significant diversification, unexpected and heavy claims, poor management and recession put paid to all that. In March 1992 the Department of Trade and Industry were informed of the parlous position, and trading in local-authority and public-sector insurance ceased.

What followed was a year-long search for a buyer. There were many false dawns, with prospective buyers appearing and disappearing. It was an extremely difficult period for those actively involved in the sale, for the possibility of insolvency and the immediate collapse of the business was ever present. Those not so involved (the great majority of employees) were more sanguine. They were simply unable to take in the possibility that a company which had been in existence for 90 years could possibly founder – even when all the signs were it was doing just that.

Some six months after putting itself up for sale, discussion with Zurich Insurance began. A further six months later a deal was concluded whereby Zurich acquired MMI's local-authority portfolio and related services, but excluding past years' claims liabilities.

On 9 March 1993, 1,600 employees transferred to Zurich Insurance. And so began a planned and meticulously carried out process to offer realistic job security while maintaining a firm hold on the business. The context was frightening: Zurich in the UK acquired as many new staff as it had previously employed, so there was an overnight doubling of staff and two very different cultures to contend with.

Communication and lots of it was essential for both employees and customers. Consistent and clear messages were absolutely vital and went a long way towards scotching the rumour machine. Zurich's policy was for open communication between all employees. Good communication channels such as team briefing, staff newspaper and E Mail were already in place, but the really effective communication was face to face. It was essential to make the newcomers feel part of Zurich and impart a sense of urgency and desire to succeed, particularly in securing the local-authority business.

Personnel played a significant part in communicating and harmonising terms and conditions of employment. Although much thought went into the process of integration, the plans saw the light of day on 9 March 1993 and were completed comfortably within the published target of the year end.

Day one was important, for it was a time for saying farewell to MMI and welcome to Zurich. The Chairman and the Chief Executive of MMI wrote to all staff transferring, and met with all the managers. Few tears were shed. It was not that kind of occasion. Rather there was an air of excitement, tinged with apprehension, an urgency for getting on and really getting back to work. Later the same day managers from both the regions and head office, fully briefed by their personnel managers, returned to their offices to brief staff. Every member of staff was presented with a pack containing welcome letters, confirming the transfer of employment, a question and answer document on terms and conditions, pension information, corporate information about the company and the staff newspaper. Everyone was given a list of names to contact if they had specific queries, and a Helpline number for non-specific issues. That worked well: many small irritations or misunderstandings were quashed before becoming serious.

Day three saw all the newcomer Managers together again to learn of Zurich, its strength, worldwide disposition, culture and 'the way we do things round here'. It was the first such meeting and was followed by many more around the country with all transferred staff. It proved a huge success in giving information and warmth to newcomers. All other communication channels were used to support the messages: special editions of the staff newspaper, E mail messages and team briefs together with a video from the CEO. But – and in hindsight it was a big but – in the concentration on the newcomers the feelings of the existing Zurich staff were overlooked. It was taken for granted they would be happy about the acquisition. Not enough thought had been given to their concerns about job security. It was a lesson learnt – at a later stage, when some redundancies became necessary, a full programme for the 'survivors' was put into place with gratifying results.

Throughout the following six months working parties chewed over and made recommendations on harmonising terms and conditions of employment. There were some hard nuts to crack, but it can be fairly stated that no employee was worse off after acquisition than he or she had been before.

A side effect of the harmonisation was to bring all personnel policies up to date. Those things 'we will sort out later' had to be sorted then and there. Today there are new staff hand-books, new pension booklets and benefit statements, clear policies on safety training, and the myriad other 'good employer' activities you would expect from a leading insurance company.

Without business the foregoing would have been somewhat academic: it is a strong flow of profitable business that keeps staff gainfully employed. Obviously we needed to act fast and decisively to secure the local-authority business. For a year the authorities had been very concerned that they might find themselves without their specialist insurer, and were already seeking alternative insurers in the market places. Insurance brokers were keen to make inroads into a market that they had signally failed to break into before. Zurich's policy was consistent with that for staff, lots of communication coupled with asking customers what they wanted. Zurich was well received. From the outset the CEO and the GM of Zurich Municipal (the business unit specialising in local authority insurance) wrote regularly to chief executives or finance directors of authorities to keep them informed of progress. Zurich Municipal business managers, sited at regional offices, maintained regular contact with the day-to-day insurance buyer in the authority. Local authority associations and pro-fessional bodies were briefed and soundings taken to ensure Zurich was providing the service required.

At an early stage a survey was commissioned to find out what it was that authorities really wanted from their insurers. Many myths and legends were destroyed in the process and a fundamental repositioning called for.

Inevitably there were redundancies. Some two hundred jobs were lost. Every effort was made to see if relocation or redeployment was an alternative, but for those where this was not possible at least six months' notice was given of the redundancy, and outplacement was offered to all.

Now, a year and a half after the acquisition, the moving in and settling down has been completed. Zurich Municipal is an integrated part of Zurich in the UK. It is pulling its weight, leaner, providing better service and has regained its respect. The cosy relationship between insurer and authority has gone; the demise of MMI was a fearful shock and its memory will not fade that quickly.

The issues now facing Zurich are softer ones, but no less important. At the most senior levels work is progressing currently on culture, bureaucracy and performance management. These are the keys to success. In today's fierce marketplace a competitive edge has to be found everywhere. The company's core values need to be identified and aligned with the needs of staff and clients in order to achieve profits and profitable growth for the shareholders.

9

Thriving on Change and Supporting the Casualties

This chapter identifies the characteristics of individuals who have the capacity for not only coping with change but also for turning a crisis into an opportunity to progress. Attention will be drawn to some important lessons on how best to support the casualties of change – particularly those who have experienced a severe degree of trauma and who therefore encounter real difficulty in getting restarted. Questions will be raised regarding the implications, for organisations, in selecting and supporting people affected by, for example, a major restructure. Certain aspects of training and support will be discussed, as will various factors which may help to identify those likely to respond best (and worst) to change.

The material presented here is based on the experience of counselling over 3,000 individuals over the past five years as well as on empirical data collected for approximately 1,000 executives. Most of the individuals concerned were referred by leading career management consultancies and outplacement agencies. Those counselled were professional and managerial staff, the majority of whom (about 80 per cent) were men.

We start by examining some significant aspects of an individual's background which may help to generate capacities for coping with change. This is followed by a consideration of related personality traits, which appear to be associated with an optimally successful response to change. Then the factors which can provide support for the 'casualties of change' are discussed. Finally, some questions are suggested which could usefully be raised by HR managers who are faced with organisational change.

Personal background factors

From analyses of the personal backgrounds of 'victims of change', there emerge some factors common to those individuals who seem able to respond to change more successfully than others. Family background and personal factors which appear to be associated with successful response include:

- *a stable and secure family base*: this begins very early in life, as suggested by Bowlby's emphasis that a positive and enduring close emotional relationship is highly beneficial during the first two years with the 'caregiver'
- *developing independence*: the ability, from an early age, to independently explore, to move away from a secure family base – for example, as demonstrated by the ease with which a person gets involved in sports, clubs and the community
- *access to a 'Significant Other(s)'*: to provide a flexible, open-minded and successful role model(s)
- *a drive to grow and develop*: such a person will probably be highly results-orientated, with a reluctance to stand still, as evidenced by willing participation in training courses and proactively managing their own career.

It is important to be clear about the difference between healthy and mal-adaptive response to change. Surprisingly, perhaps, a person with a background of insecurity may be more likely to initiate personal change than someone from a more secure background. In terms of the model or successful change response, it is important to have both the early experience of moving away and exploring *and* the simultaneous confidence in the availability of a stable and supportive family base.

Thus a person who – as a child – experienced insecure change might well become *psychologically addicted to change*. An example of insecure change might be a too-early experience of boarding school, together with the perception that the family was not really there to support and care for the child (perhaps because of living abroad). It has been noted that people who had such experiences as children are often unable, or less able, to form close emotional relationships as adults and may show a tendency to hop from one relationship (and/or job) to another. Such people, however, may be attracted to what they see as supportive organisations – the forces, institutions, large corporate organisations, and so on. Here we may see the formal nature of 'structured' support provided without any risk of emotional involvement (and of being subsequently 'let down').

This is not necessarily all bad news for organisations. Indeed – as with other similar motivators, such as, for example, the need for recognition and approval which can result in high personal achievement drive – this factor can be channelled into achieving a high level of business results. When, however, such a profile becomes 'pathological', then it may be counter-productive: for instance, when premature change is activated, the effects may include lack of completion and follow-through, which could weaken team cohesiveness.

In an ideal world, those with a healthy response to change will be more content personally and so will those around them (colleagues, friends, family) too. An HR manager who identifies a mal-adaptive change pattern would therefore be well advised to direct the individual into counselling to explore aspects of his/her behaviour in response to change, and in particular how best to handle this personal crisis and its organisational implications.

Personality factors affecting a successful response to change

The results which follow are drawn from a statistical analysis of over 1,000 individuals who had undergone psychometric assessment of their personal characteristics. Tests were used to help identify strengths and weaknesses in relation to both their fit with the various job options being considered and also certain aspects of their self-marketing.

The results of two personality questionnaires (the Sixteen Personality Factor Questionnaire and the SHL Occupational Personality Questionnaire) were matched statistically with other data on the 'occupational success' of newly redundant executives. This sample was a good sized sub-set of the initial sample, for whom complete and reliable data could be obtained on their job-seeking success. The criteria used for 'occupational success' were

- the time taken to find a new job
- the increase (or decrease) in salary level over their previous job.

It was hypothesised that a successful response to being made redundant could be indicated by a quick entry into a new job and also by obtaining an increased benefit package. The aim of the study was to examine the 'personality correlates' of job success.

For those less familiar with psychometric assessment techniques, the 16PF is a multi-trait personality questionnaire based on original factor analytic research by Professor Ray Cattell and his team, in the 1950s. It has been widely researched and used all over the world, and has acquired a wide range of supportive data from academics and practitioners alike. The OPQ was developed by British occupational psychologists Saville and Holdsworth, and is a slightly more occupationally relevant, if rather more transparent, instrument than the 16PF. Both questionnaires are self-report type inventories, requiring candidates to choose between multiple-choice items or questions to which their responses are then rated according to a series of scales. Typically, the full-length versions (of the 16PF and the OPQ) each take about 45 minutes to complete. Such duration is necessary in order to be both comprehensive and accurate in estimating a range of relevant personality dimensions.

Although there are a number of different personality models available, there is common agreement nowadays that most 'respectable' tests measure aspects of the 'Big Five' personality dimensions. These, in turn, are:

- **extraversion** – *versus* – **introversion**
- **high anxiety** – *versus* – **low anxiety/mental stability**
- **tough poise** – *versus* – **emotionality** (openness to experience)
- **independence** – *versus* – **conformity**
- **conscientiousness** – *versus* – **low control**.

The 16PF provides an accurate assessment of these five 'secondary personality factors' and gives a detailed description in terms of sixteen 'source trait' or primary factors. A brief description of these dimensions may help to rectify the misleading stereotypes popularly associated with these labels.

An **extravert** (spelt with an *a* by psychologists!) is not simply the party-going, loud and jokey, character who is commonly associated with that word. For psychologists, being a 'hail fellow, well met' type may be part of the picture, but the notion of 'extraversion' possesses some other, less well known, meanings. Unpacking 'extraversion', we find that it is a composite of being *outgoing*, having *social confidence*, being *uninhibited* and *good at making* and *maintaining social contacts*. Generally, an extravert is someone who is 'out there' dealing with the world (as well as being people-orientated), in contrast to the introvert, who is more self-sufficient, shy, inhibited, more introspective and inward-looking.

The **anxiety** factor corresponds more closely with what is commonly thought of as 'being anxious' – those described by this factor as stable (i.e. less anxious) tend to be more satisfied with their lives and are relatively capable of achieving their goals as compared with those people with very high levels of anxiety, which can be inhibiting. Similarly, someone very low on anxiety may be described as 'laid-back' and lacking in urgency. The well known 'inverted U' curve (Figure 9.1) describes this dimension, with an optimum response being

Figure 9.1
The 'inverted U' curve

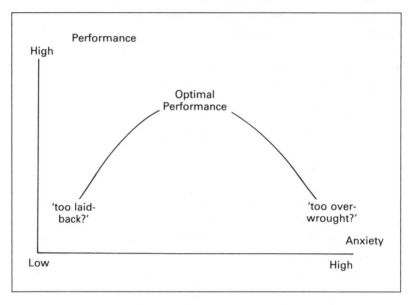

somewhere between the two extremes – depending on the circumstances and the individual.

Tough poise (*versus* **emotional** sensitivity) is another commonly misunderstood factor. 'Toughness' is generally thought of as a 'good thing' in business, but what is being assessed by this factor is a composite of artistic and cultural sensitivity, interest in people, and sensitivity to one's own feelings as well as to those of others. High scorers on tough poise are relatively pragmatic, interested in data or 'things', and hard-headed – sometimes even to the extent of being insensitive to the feelings of others.

Independence is a relatively straightforward factor: it is about being assertive, being unlikely to be swayed by group opinion and being likely to have strong views. **Conformists**, on the other hand, are more likely to want to achieve a consensus and will be flexible, perhaps to the extent of not knowing their own minds.

Finally, high scorers on **conscientiousness** (or **control**) will tend to be dutiful, rule following, with a high tolerance for detail and structure. Those working in compliance areas, including law and finance, tend to score high on control. Low scorers tend to feel constrained by rules and structure, and lean towards expedient solutions and approaches. City traders and entrepreneurs, for example, tend to score low on control, and are typically more spontaneous – though less self-disciplined – than high scorers.

Findings from psychometric testing and other studies

Statistical analysis of the psychometric data, together with the outcomes of our analysis of the personal background factors, revealed that the more successful executives tended to be significantly more:

- intelligent
- extraverted
- stable (less anxious)
- open to experience and more agreeable (lower on tough poise)

than their less successful colleagues.

Put another way, those who secured new jobs more quickly (and those who received better benefit packages) were generally more outgoing, were better adjusted emotionally, were more open to new ideas and were more people-centred.

Intuitively, one is tempted to think that 'When the going gets tough, its the tough who get going.' Perhaps, however, we need to redefine 'tough', because this study suggests the opposite – that when the going gets tough, it is the sensitive and open who are more effective at responding to change. Here, as previously defined, 'tough' means 'hard headed' and more 'thing- or data-minded' than people-centred.

So, being more open and more innovative (and intelligent), the more successful executives tend to be better at exploring new options and at evaluating themselves in relation to their past and present situations. Being better adjusted emotionally, they are more resilient, and better able to cope with stress and rejection. Finally, being more extraverted and people-centred, they tend to get along well with others, and are probably able to sell themselves more effectively.

Assessment of change competence

There is growing evidence, from sources other than those drawn upon already, that the 'Big Five' personality factors can help to identify occupational success in many spheres. For most work-related purposes, however, it may be that sharper focus is required than the broad brush strokes which this model allows. For this reason, personality questionnaires, whose coverage affords greater depth and detail, are generally used for career counselling and selection purposes. Thus, specialised psychometric tools may be especially helpful (and more powerful) when used in conjunction with other techniques – such as focused behavioural interviewing – in order to assess change competence.

How can we identify and assess individuals who will respond well to change? Indeed, how can we also identify those who may require extra help and support in coping with change?

The 'state-of-the-art' these days, of course, involves using psychometric tests and measures *together with* the use of specialised interviewing techniques. What is important is *which* type of tests are used, *how* they are used and *how this information is integrated* with the other data in relation to a useful competency model.

Focused interviews, using behavioural evidence to support judgements, can overcome major problems of subjectivity and bias in interviews. Moreover, reliable and appropriate tests (which have been proven to be consistent and accurate) need to be interpreted in the light of additional evidence. It has been stated elsewhere in this book that psychometric tests will capture only the *surface traits* – those which an individual knows about him or herself and is prepared to share with the assessor. This information may, therefore, need to be supplemented by an in-depth psychological counselling interview. Over and above this, time spent in explaining clearly why the assessment is being carried out, and in building trust between assessor and candidate, will increase the value of the whole exercise.

We should be clear at this stage that what we have been exploring are the qualities associated with successful *response to change*, as distinct from those qualities required for successful *change leadership potential*. The notion of 'change leadership' relates to a step further on from a successful 'change response'. It seems to us that managers of the future may need to go beyond making successful responses to change, and proactively recognise the need for change and initiating new areas of change which, previously, may not have been recognised. The qualities associated with identifying and developing 'change leadership potential' are discussed more fully in Chapter 13.

The casualties of change

If these findings show us who are likely to be the most *and* the least successful at responding to change, two main questions arise:

Firstly, why are organisations letting go of some of their best people? Surely enormous amounts of human resource potential are being wasted by careless selection of candidates for redundancy?

Secondly, what about those individuals who are less successful? What support and development would help them to cope more successfully with a change crisis?

The casualties of change can thus be seen to include both those individuals whose careers may be temporarily disrupted and also those organisations who may be wasting significant potential.

The term 'trauma' can cover several distinct stages of shock experienced by 'casualties of change'. Trauma is usually a response to loss of some kind – a job or perhaps bereavement. It is important to distinguish these various stages, and HR and line managers will need to be able to recognise them, as will the individuals themselves. They are part of a 'normal' reaction to crisis and change, although the timing and severity of these stages will vary from one individual to another.

Shock is the initial response to loss, and the event can be either blown up out of proportion or else trivialised during this stage. Severe mood swings are a possibility, ranging between immobilisation and elation. In the next stage, the individual feels generally depressed, although mood swings continue. Then, after a period of adjustment, and with the necessary support, the individual begins to learn to cope, and mood swings tend to stabilise. Gradually and eventually, the person returns to 'normal', although particular stages may repeat themselves without warning.

Our concern now is with individuals as 'casualties' of change, and with the means of support that are likely to be available to them.

Support and lifestyle

We might divide the support available for an individual undergoing stressful change into:

- that which the individual him or herself provides
- personal support which may be provided by friends and family, and
- formal support provided by the organisation or by a third party, say, by an external counsellor or an agency.

One important form of **self-support** within the immediate

reach of most people is a lifestyle which enables a potentially highly stressful situation to be managed more effectively. This means healthy living, attention to diet (especially avoiding excessive use of alcohol), and physical fitness. Depending on the outcome of an audit of these factors, professional advice may be sought. What is imperative is for steps to be taken to find a healthful balance between work, play and rest.

An individual's **personal support** would be provided by a resilient and supportive family and/or partner, and, of course, friends. Additional personal support may be sought from rather more formal agencies such as mentors, counsellors, masseurs, fitness consultants, GP, and so on.

Formal support would be provided by the organisation itself. This may come internally via HR managers, trainers, counsellors or mentors, or externally via EAP (Employee Assistance Programme) counsellors, career consultants, trainers, mentors, outplacement agencies, and so on.

After an assessment of needs, counselling support needs to focus on the likely deficit areas which can be addressed or made more acceptable. Some factors can be addressed through training, for example, enhancing interpersonal skills. Other factors, such as high anxiety levels, may require specialist counselling support in order for an individual to come to terms with and to accept her or his situation more readily. Occupational counselling may help an individual to achieve a career goal through a combination of skills training and support, or it may help to clarify career goals and so re-direct an individual's job search.

Our study of successful job-seekers suggests that support for the less successful may prove most beneficial by addressing such areas as:

- developing interpersonal sensitivity and flexibility
- assertiveness training
- self-marketing skills development and support
- counselling support for anxiety and confidence related issues
- stress management support and training.

Summary and conclusions

The key features of those who are likely to successfully respond to and manage change include:

- a secure family background
- mobility and independence
- emotional balance, resilience and good health
- intelligence, creativity, and openness to new possibilities
- people-centredness
- proactivity
- effective personal and formal support.

Through a combination of psychometric assessment and focused interviewing, we can identify both those who will probably deal successfully with change and also those who may encounter rather more difficulty. This raises questions concerning organisational responsibility for providing the necessary support for those individuals who cope less successfully with personal crisis.

Finally, studies have repeatedly shown that the most able are quickly snapped up by the job market, sometimes by their previous employer, following a generous redundancy settlement and, sometimes, a lucrative period of freelance consultancy.

So why do some organisations let some of their best staff go? Apart from short-term economic motives (which analysis of the re-employment rates of redundant executives suggests may well be misguided), the explanation may in part concern the problems associated with identifying those who will best be able to cope with change. Equally important, and rather more challenging, however, are issues involving the role and influence of the HR function, which are discussed elsewhere in this book. Ultimately, the solution may hinge on how well HR professionals can present cost/benefit arguments to financially-orientated managers.

Some questions for HR managers to ask

1 Are we clear about which characteristics are associated with a successful *response to change*?

2 Are we clear about the differences between healthy and maladaptive change response patterns?

3 Can we identify and assess the qualities associated with both successful and less successful *change responses*?

4 Can we identify and assess the qualities associated with *change leadership potential*?

5 Can we assess the extent of an individual's need for support?

6 Are we wasting our best talent i.e. making redundant those best able to thrive on change?

7 What are the implications for overall HRD strategies and policies if we anticipate that we are likely to be faced with change, re-structuring and adaption?

8 What is the role and influence of the HR function in the management of change arena?

9 How clear are we about the cost/benefit issues affecting staff turnover, marginal improvements in performance, etc?

References

Bowlby, J. *A Secure Base: Clinical Application of Attachment Theory*, Tavistock/Routledge (1988)

Brindle, L.R. 'How executives get better jobs (more quickly)' *Journal of Managerial Psychology*, **7** (3), 17–22 (1992)

Cattell, R.B. *Handbook for the Sixteen Personality Factor Questionnaire*. ASE/NFER-Nelson Windsor, U.K. (1970)

Saville, P. *Manual for the Occupational Personality Questionnaire*. SHL: Esher (1990)

10

Managing the new Manager

Introduction

The authors of this chapter, Ashley Wood and Paul Henry, have worked together in various capacities related to selection and development. Ashley Wood is Personnel Development Manager at Meyer International, a distributor of construction materials. Paul Henry is an HR consultant from ODL who works with Meyer International and other UK and international organisations. His background is occupational psychology.

We have often found ourselves reflecting on our own experiences of developing as young managers in the work environment and considering the experiences of current young managers entering organisations. The subject is of course close to our hearts as the people responsible for the selection, training and development of individuals in the 'real world'.

Like many other organisations, over the past few years, Meyer International has experienced much change. Some of it has been welcomed and some of it has still to be confronted and dealt with. Restructuring to create a flatter and more responsive company structure has been a necessity, rather than a merely fashionable thing to do.

We had come to the realisation recently that we had a problem of succession in one of the group's key divisions. This division had a real need of young people with ability and strong management potential. Meyer International has, therefore, invested considerable resources and energy into a scheme for developing the new manager in the organisation.

Introducing new managers to an organisation with a strong tradition of 'growth from within' has presented a number of challenges to all involved – from the new managers themselves to the existing workforce, the line and senior management, and of course the HR team.

'Managing the new manager' is however, something to which we are committed on a personal as well as a professional level. We are aware that it is an area about which our thoughts are continually developing.

Later in the chapter, we describe eight principles by which we operate when managing the new manager. These principles have been recently applied to a scheme which was set up to address the succession issue previously mentioned. We have moved from one situation, in which there was considerable resistance to bringing young managers into the division from the outside, to another, in which we are having difficulty keeping up with the demands from middle and senior management for 'more of those young managers'. The benefit which managers saw was that the new mangers were able to contribute almost immediately by generating new solutions to old problems. This can be largely attributed to the fact that the eight principles allow the new managers to learn quickly, by taking advantage of wisdom crystallised in the organisation, while at the same time allowing them to demonstrate and apply their talent from the start.

Defining 'empowerment' through experience

There is a large body of theory concerning young managers and empowerment which is espoused by numerous companies and management gurus, and which features in the professional literature. Much of this theorising we find to be repetitive and circular in reasoning. In planning this chapter, therefore, we decided to put all this to one side and to approach our subject instead from our experience of what worked for us and, it seems, the young managers being developed at Meyer International.

Our starting point was to consider what 'empowerment' meant to us. After a somewhat convoluted conversation, we found ourselves reaching for *The Oxford English Dictionary*, where we found a simple definition which read: 'to authorise, to enable'. This expressed our own understanding very well.

We then considered our own experiences of developing in new working environments, recalling situations which have been significantly empowering and others which were quite the reverse. We agreed that, in some contexts, we had felt initially empowered, only later to understand that some systems and some people within them will react to the point of actually *disempowering* others who adopted their values less rigidly. Slowly but surely the system and the people had taught us on a deep level the rules of the game and the way 'things are done around here'.

It also seemed to us, in reflecting upon colleagues over the years, that there are some people who are prone to becoming disempowered. Perhaps the question should therefore be not only, how do we empower people, but also how do we stop them becoming disempowered?

We are born empowered. It runs deeper within a person than just being enabled or authorised to respond within the organisational context. So this question of empowerment is as relevant in the home as it is in the community, the education system, and within organisations, Empowerment is a quality which is within all of us, to some degree. Either it has been allowed to flourish or it has been oppressed. Therefore, some young people arrive at our organisations with their energy and sense of empowerment vibrantly intact, while others arrive after having 'learned' the lesson of helplessness.

The simile that we heard being used by a senior manager recently was that empowering people was sometimes like taking the pot off of a plant. Unless the roots are teased out from their moulded shape, they will stay bound in the form that had restrained them for so long. Some people are equipped to take the pot off themselves. Some people need to be helped to find their true potential. But it is important to remember that empowerment is ultimately something that people develop themselves under the right conditions.

The challenge for organisations, then, is to provide an

environment which will re-kindle, harness and nurture this natural spirit of empowerment in young people.

Principles for managing new managers

The following are the fundamental principles which we follow in dealing with any young manager at work. You will probably recognise them as common sense: we hope that you do. Our experience is, however, that they are not commonly practised.

1. Empower yourself

When attempting to provide an empowering environment for another person, it is first necessary to consider two matters: firstly, the extent to which you as a manager are enabled and authorised to do so by your organisation; and secondly, and perhaps more importantly, how empowered you feel yourself to be.

If you think that you cannot empower young people beneath you because you do not possess either the influence or the authority, or because the culture is non-conducive, we would ask you to consider the following:

- We are all constrained to some degree by the nature of our organisations. If your focus of attention is on what you cannot achieve, you always will find reasons not to try new solutions. On the other hand if you concentrate on you current sphere of influence, you will find that this will shift your focus to what *is* possible. Over time, you will find that your sphere of influence will grow.
- Very often, we construct our own boundaries to beliefs, which we base on our interpretation of previous experience. It is useful for us to question and test what we believe to be true concerning our level of freedom within the organisation.

- If the first two recommendations seem too difficult, the principle, that 'it is easier to ask for forgiveness than it is to ask for permission,' often achieves results.

2. Find ways to dovetail the needs of the organisation with those of the individual

The trend towards creating flatter structures for organisations has an important consequence for the young manager, in that the traditional career path for people with ability is no longer, necessarily, *up* the corporate ladder. Managers are more likely to spend longer at each level, while faced with increasing odds against them achieving promotion to the next level up.

This altered situation requires that managers at each level become more responsive than previously to the needs of individual young managers. Because of the uniqueness of each person, it is necessary to be equally creative and flexible in dovetailing individual with business needs.

This will entail providing those conditions for the development of young managers that help them to evolve at the personal level, to develop their identity, values and beliefs. In doing so, the young manager is growing in ways which are of deep value to the organisation, as well as to themselves.

3. Get the right people in and be honest with what you promise

One of the most common complaints we have heard from young people is that the company where they work promised them *this* level of involvement and *that* level of responsibility, neither of which had subsequently materialised. This had lowered morale and, in some cases, actually influenced the decision to quit the company.

Managers manifestly should not promise what they cannot deliver. Instead, people should be given the story straight – they will appreciate it, whether or not they decide to join the organisation.

Look at what 'empowerment' means to your organisation in real terms. Take a look at your values and communicate them to potential recruits. Make sure that their values, generally, are aligned with those of your organisation. Pay attention to what the company *really* values rather than what it says that it values. Actions have their roots in values.

Do as much as you can to ensure that your organisation can meet the expectations of people. Young managers, who have had little, if any, experience of being seduced by a tantalising company line which has not subsequently become reality, are prone to developing false expectations.

4. Choose their environment carefully

Consider the professional boxer and his manager: the boxer's manager is careful to hand-pick his novice's contests, each contest providing the boxer with the necessary challenge and requisite learning for the next fight. A hard fight too early on can lose (to use the boxing term) the fighter's 'heart': if the contest is overwhelming, the boxer can learn that defeat is perhaps not that bad at all perhaps inevitable. Look around your organisation to find the managers that have really developed young people and who will give them a proper fighting chance.

Put young managers in the least bureaucratic and autocratic parts of the organisation, at least for the first year or so. Later on, after some significant experience of working in a part of an organisation that 'authorises and enables' people, put them to meaningful work in another part of the organisation, one that could benefit from a prospective champion. Help them to develop the 'heart of a champion'. Later on, these people will be the champions of your organisation.

5. Allow them to contribute as soon as possible

Flatter structures mean that accountability and responsibility are pushed further down the organisation. It is therefore

inevitable that young people in industry today are receiving a
fair share of accountability and responsibility earlier than their
predecessors. This is a good thing, of course, but it means that
organisations need to provide preparation for such responsibility earlier in a young person's career.

Start as out you intend to carry on. From day one, ask for
new managers' opinions about your organisation and the way
you run your department. Ask for their ideas – very often the
least experienced eyes and ears can see and hear things which
we don't or which we take for granted.

Provide them with worthwhile projects and the resources to
solve real business problems. Allow them access to influential
people in the organisation for guidance and for introductions
to other like-minded people. This will help them to develop a
wisdom that could otherwise take them years of climbing the
corporate ladder. Get them to report and discuss their findings
with you. If they are right and their recommendations will
improve your company's performance, implement them; then
reward and publicise their achievements. If, however, you are
unable to put their ideas into action, explain your reasons. This
is an aspect of sound management which is, surprisingly,
frequently overlooked.

If you want to empower young people, you will have to take
them seriously and treat them as fully fledged members of the
organisation. They are your employees of today, as well as
tomorrow, and not just youngsters who need to learn a few
(hard) lessons about the 'real world' before they can start
'earning their corn'. How many times have you heard a similar
comment, even from HR professionals?

6. Provide them with regular feedback

Set up regular opportunities for you to discuss their progress
and performance. Involve them in assessment of themselves.
Foster the belief that every experience they have is an
opportunity to learn. In this way people are more likely to
experiment and evolve.

7. Remember what it was like when you first joined an organisation

Remind yourself often of who and what it was that most empowered you. Who was it that was a real source of inspiration for you, when you were just entering the organisational world? Bring them to mind when dealing with young people, particularly when you get stuck or if you suspect that you are sounding like someone who disempowered you in the past.

Bring some inspirational person to mind, and ask yourself how they would deal with young people in this situation. In this way you will be passing on a legacy of wisdom which, probably, will be passed on when your empowered young people become the champions for tomorrow's champions.

8. Maintain a sense of humour

We know of no better catalyst for bringing a sense of proportion and hope to situations. Laughter is a great reliever, and, besides, shouldn't our work also be fun?

If you have problems with this one try number 7 again.

11

Rebuilding Trust

The price of change

Throughout our book, we have developed and illustrated the notion of 'empowering change'. The message which emerges is that to achieve this standard of excellence is tough and demanding. However carefully management plans its actions, there will invariably be consequences which have not been anticipated, and which can impinge on the relationships between people at all levels. Change often, if not always, forces people to see themselves as 'winners or losers'.

Change is driven by management action, and will, at some stage, put management's philosophy, strategies and behaviour under the microscope. For example, in times of rationalisation, when company restructuring and downsizing are coupled with redundancy and redeployment programmes, people will unquestionably feel at risk, whether or not they plan to remain with the company. At such times, much of management's energy and HR's attention is given to the leavers. For the stayers, a major issue is whether or not they can really trust management not to repeat the process, if tough times reappear.

Many of the foundations of trust are put at risk in times of necessary change: business strength and health, future career options, management's openness and its real attitudes towards people, will all seem threatened by the hazards of change. For the empowering manager, the challenge is to accept that basic trust is at risk and to set about repairing and rebuilding mutual confidence.

Rebuilding trust and mutual confidence

An analysis of 'trust'

For the individual, trust is a defining quality of relationships with other people.

Where trust exists, an individual feels at one with colleagues and the total working environment.

Where it is lacking, suspicion, misunderstanding, second guessing can become the norm. The individual can feel isolated and cautious in relationships with others. The full potential of the individual's contribution can be substantially diminished.

For a manager and his team, trust is the life blood of team performance.

Where trust exists, the team can feel vigorous, confident, open, challenging and successful.

Where it is lacking, the manager's role, authority and influence are at risk. Communication is questioned, double meanings and hidden agendas are sought. Commitment to action is inhibited, and willingness to solve problems co-operatively constrained. Team performance drops.

For the organisation, trust is the core around which the corporate mission and purpose are achieved.

Where it exists, teams function effectively and collaborate, unquestioningly, with each other. Energy is focused on the external market place, and the organisation responds more quickly and creatively to market change. Competitive advantage is secured.

Where it is lacking, teamworking is inhibited, because teams treat each other with suspicion. Energy is consumed on internal politics, speculation, rumour mongering and second guessing. Management's role and credibility is questioned.

Responsiveness to market change is slowed, and quality and service can diminish. Scapegoating and witch hunting can emerge. Competitors in the market start to win, while confidence internally is eroded.

The value of trust is evident and considerable.

Where it exists, a 'win/win' for all can be achieved; where it is lacking, a 'lose/lose' environment is created.

For organisations where trust is broken, a major campaign to rebuild it is immediately essential.

If trust is so important, what really is it?

It is a **feeling**, which is influenced by: *behaviour* and *communication* between people over time.

Feelings are reactions, emotional and cerebral, experienced by and between people. Their intensity indicates the degree to which people feel good or bad about each other. Feelings can function as a measure of the match between your individual needs and values, and your expectations of others and of their behaviours and responses through time. You feel good if they are met and bad if they are denied or threatened.

To be trusted and to give trust, our feelings about each other need to be consistent over time, and their durability allows us to predict, to varying extents, how we are likely to feel in the future.

Behaviour is what we do and how we do it. Our behaviour determines, in large part, how we are perceived by others. Trust grows out of a consistency of behaviour over time. It is often destroyed when behaviours no longer fit the patterns which we expect and value.

Consistency of behaviour is the key to being trusted. Verbal and non-verbal behaviour need to display consistency. The behaviour of the 'whole' person will be monitored and assessed by others. Significant changes in behaviour can threaten the trust which characterises a relationship.

Communication is the means by which people interact. For any communication to be perceived as trustworthy, it has to be matched by behaviour, body language and sincerity. Insincere behaviour will frustrate the quality and effectiveness of the communication.

Trust in communication emanates from both what is heard and how it is interpreted. With trust, open communication and full listening will occur. Communication will become a 'two way' process.

The breakdown of trust

The risks to trust – rationalisation and redundancy

Trust takes time to build. It is borne of consistency and the quality relationships. Trust can easily be destroyed.

The recent business environment, with its continuous emphasis on survival and short term business performance, together with increased competition and market volatility has forced management into an era of downsizing, rationalisation, restructuring and redundancy. Trust has been put at risk by the drive for decisive, tough minded management action.

Downsizing can have disruptive effects on an organisation's personnel:

- behaviour is changed
- expectations are not fulfilled
- relationships become ambiguous
- conflict between roles emerge.

The situation has the potential for becoming anomic, with the expected norms of behaviour ignored.

Confronting alternatives

Important and difficult choices confront both management and personnel in situations of necessary downsizing.

For the manager, the alternatives are *either* to persist with his normal style, *or* to stand back from people and assume a detached, tough minded position. This choice will determine the nature of the risk to the trust relationship.

In a climate of frequent change, members of staff will experience heightened sensitivity and increased anticipation of problems and difficulties. They will look to their manager to behave in a consistent way, but may be faced with a 'changed' individual. To trust or not to trust is the difficult choice confronting them. The seeds of mistrust are easily sown.

Rebuilding or repairing trust

Change within organisations invariably results in ambiguity and uncertainty. But is the confusion which emerges indicative of a breakdown in trust or of a denting of trust?

How do we decide whether trust has been damaged or broken?

There are no clinical diagnostic tests by which unarguable conclusions may be deduced in this area. There are various relevant factors, however, which can usefully be considered when trying to gauge the extent of the damage done.

Defining the basis of trust

The critical influences on trust within organisations include:

- the quality of line managers' relations with staff

- the quality of peer relationships
- team expectations and fears
- the effectiveness of company communication processes
- management's style, policies and practices in dealing with people
- current company performance
- company standing and image in the local community, the national press and the general business community
- organisational climate and culture.

In rebuilding trust, it is essential to identify those factors which most influence trust. The wider the range of influences at work, the more extensive the rebuilding required; the more focused the influences, the greater the chance of successful repair.

The target groups

In formulating a rebuilding strategy, it is important for senior management to identify the potential 'opinion formers' within the company. Once these groups and individuals have been targeted, management should initiate a series of meetings the objects of which are to demonstrate a willingness to listen and to take account of their views, and to co-opt them in the process of rebuilding. Given the influence of these groups and individuals, their involvement in the rebuilding process will lay the foundation for a 'critical mass' of support.

Another vital group will consist of those most directly affected by change. A willingness to involve them in the programme of change implementation would strengthen the foundations of the rebuilding process.

It is important, also, to enlist the support of 'the change policy and practices influencers' in the organisation, among whom would be the HR personnel. They would be capable of detecting further trust problems and issues, and also of contributing significantly to the determination of policies and practices to be followed in rebuilding trust.

Measuring damage

It is important to decide, early on in the rebuilding process,
upon the means by which the extent of the damage to
organisational trust is to be estimated. Options here would
include

- interviews
- questionnaires
- group discussions.

A combination of all three may well prove most effective.

Although important visible indicators will be afforded by
changes in management and staff behaviour, there are likely to
be questions about the objectivity of recording and reporting
methods. Data gathered in this informal manner may, however, be used in relation to data from other sources.

Questionnaires can be developed which enable management
to assess whether they have a 'trust problem'. Anonymnity can
help to ensure reliable feedback. Interviews and group discussion can explore the deep seated feelings and frustrations.
Skilled facilitators will be needed, and confidentiality safe-
guarded in all instances.

In analysing the returned information, it will be necessary to
take due account of sample size and statistical substance.

The success of the data gathering exercise will largely
depend upon the extent of trust placed by respondents on the
process. Any feeling that it is a cosmetic exercise will reinforce
the breakdown of trust which measures such as this are
attempting to rectify.

Launching a 'trust rebuilding project'

Great care will be needed in the positioning and communication of any project at such a time. A positioning with a focus on
'learning from change', rather than on 'facing up to morale and

trust problems', would be beneficial. A significant strategic choice would be whether to go for a major campaign/project aimed at the workforce, or whether to pursue a programme of management education leading to individual managers taking actions within their own teams. A management philosophy statement of 'willingness to learn from each other' could, if perceived as sincere, demonstrate that management really cares. The option of rebuilding by osmosis could leave pockets of resistance, maybe linked to those areas of management insensitivity where the trust problems reside.

Any communication would need to be carefully planned to ensure, as far as possible, that it is 'trustworthy'. Important questions in the planning would include:

- 'Is it in a form that all levels can comprehend?'
- 'Have the expectations of the recipients been fully understood and accepted?'
- 'Can management ensure that the expectations will be met?'

Raised expectations, followed by a delayed or limited response, could reinforce rather than improve the situation.

Manager behaviour

If the aim is to initiate a management-led exercise, then those managers involved must understand that it is *their* behaviour which will influence trust most decisively. Influential factors here will include their

- sensitivity to their impact on others
- sincerity in presenting 'trustworthy' messages
- willingness and ability to 'actively listen'
- capacity to deal with challenge and feedback in a 'non-defensive' way.

It is vital that the 'trust rebuilders' have the appropriate qualities and skills. Careful selection is essential and training workshops may well be needed. Any upward feedback and team review processes may require the involvement of a skilled facilitator.

Auditing the management competences needed to build trust

If a major, company-wide exercise is planned, it may be advisable to devise an 'audit' on whether or not senior management inspire trust. The judgement, as to whether the development of 'trust building competences' is vital to future organisational performance, would need to come from the project steering group.

Such a management audit could encompass questions concerning management's

- values
- underlying motives
- capability to empathise
- levels of sensitivity
- tolerance of ambiguity
- degrees of emotional control
- affiliation needs.

The emphasis would be on current management competences and whether they are sufficient to build a 'trusting organisation'. The 'audit' would follow the normal practice of a competency intervention. It would involve a mixture of questionnaires and interviews, with each individual manager's interview lasting around three hours. Individuals would be counselled on how they can become successful 'managers of trust'. Role plays and workshops could also be involved.

A 'trust rebuilding' strategy

The rebuilding strategy would need to recognise the different requirements of the various levels of the organisation.

*At the **junior** levels,* the requirements are likely to pre-dominantly concern affiliation. People need to feel valued and to belong. Their key reference points will be their own teams and immediate working environment.

Effective interventions here would relate to team building and future work planning.

*At the **middle management** levels,* the main requirement is likely to concern individual empowerment and personal achievement. This group could be the keystone around which any strategy is developed. Interventions here would focus on empowerment, and would aim to address the systems, procedures and practices which will need to change to allow management freedom of action. They will need to address the roles and relationships with senior management. Management team reviews targeted on the freedom and support needed by middle management would also help. Upward feedback sessions, aimed at 'negotiating' the changed relationships needed, respectively, 'between the boss and the team' and 'between team players', would be productive. The focus could be 'our team, its' role and influence within the changed organisation'.

An investment in managers at this level would be a demonstration of the value placed on them. Training and development could begin with exercises on 'middle management competences for success in our new organisation', and would lead to individual development plans, and issue in:

- influencing skills training
- teambuilding training
- staff coaching and counselling skills.

*At the **senior management** levels,* the requirement is likely to be the rebuilding of credibility and authority.

Interventions at this level are likely to involve personal counselling and advice. They could be focused around an exercise to determine 'director level competences for the future', in which case the aim would be to provide counsel regarding the personal leadership strategies to be followed.

The culture of the 'top team' would also be an important consideration. If the team was open and willing to learn, then direct interventions could be considered, such as 'leading our business through an era of continuous and frequent change'. This could encompass individual data gathering on

- the lessons from the changes made to date
- team strengths/weaknesses
- the major future business challenges
- the leadership philosophy and strategy required to rebuild confidence, morale and performance.

A director level workshop to formulate 'an agenda for change' might produce significant contributions to the rebuilding process.

If the team was conservative and somewhat closed, then an individual counselling approach, concentrating an 'team interventions and initiatives', would probably be more effective.

To succeed, such a 'trust rebuilding' strategy as is outlined here would need to be forward looking. The aim would be to provide the appropriate competences, processes and relationships for future organisational success. A positioning of the initiative in relation to 'the business/market challenges into the future' and 'our management and organisational response' would serve to make the energy focus outwards, rather than inwards.

Summary – a potential programme for action

The actions which could comprise a 'trust rebuilding' strategy are:

A top team intervention: either at the director level or at the functional team level, which would need to be driven by the

HR function and would focus on the consequences of 'mistrust' on overall performance; the aim would be to seek top management support for a planned intervention.

Communicating the need: a 'steering group' should be formed to launch the campaign and to consider the overall plan of action.

Diagnosing the problems: options here would be questionnaires, interviews and team discussions with vital 'target groups'.

Enhancing management skills: a series of management workshops aimed at developing the capabilities of management to handle the issues involved in rebuilding trust.

A management competencies exercise: to realign 'managing trust' as a core competence for future management success, achievable through the fulfillment of individual development plans.

A strategy of phased interventions:
- at the *junior* level, involving
  - team building
  - future work planning
  - job/work redesign
- at the *middle* level, involving
  - empowerment exercises
  - team role negotiation and mutual support for the future
  - team feedback sessions
  - competency/individual development exercises
  - programmes to enhance skills in influencing, team building, counselling and coaching
- at the *senior* level, involving
  - director level counselling
  - director level competencies for the future
  - top team workshops

    – individual counselling on leadership philosophies and
    strategies

The role, influence and competences of the HR team: specific
interventions here could include:

- HR team workshops on the strategies needed to 'rebuild
  trust and mutual confidence'
- reviews of HR policies and practices relating to change
- team reviews on the future role and influence of HR in
  planning change.

12

Judging the Individual's Capacity to Change

Endemic organisational change, if it is to be responded to proactively and successfully, requires individuals who have the capability to manage both themselves and their environment effectively. Management frequently makes decisions about the capacity of individuals for change, generally or specifically. Management decides, when an individual applies for a position, if the person matches the requirements of the job. Judgements are made about an individual's capabilities in respect of promotion, transfer and development. All such decisions take account of the elements of change which are involved in lateral and upward career moves; and management's judgements are made on the basis of an assessment of an individual's capacity for exhibiting the skills, knowledge and attitudes required by the new and/or future (changed) role.

Critical questions can be asked in respect of HR and line managers' capabilities to define the role, the team and organisational dimensions of the job, and to judge the capabilities of the individual in respect of their requirements.

Defining the role

Most HR professionals will have learned or been taught some form of job analysis. The majority will have learned to produce job descriptions and accountability statements. How many of them, though, are critically aware of the methods they use and the utility of those methods in a changing environment? How many HR departments regularly update their descriptions of jobs, teams and organisation? Even more fundamental is the question of the usefulness of description when the likelihood is that in a flatter, more matrix structure, the identification of lines of authority and responsibility, lists of duties and relationships might be difficult if not impossible. But assuming that HR wishes, for whatever reason (perhaps to fulfil the needs of a salary system) to have job descriptions, then there should be frequent (no less than every six months) auditing and rewriting of these 'Tablets of Stone'. The image seems to be apposite. They may well be the relics of those who died as followers of the 'formal' process, slaves to a system which demands formalisation. Job descriptions may empower HR, but they can also restrict organisational effectiveness.

The principal need may well be to understand the person. What motivates him? How does she think about issues? Is he tactical or visionary? Is she innovatory, or does she focus down? Does he seek to influence through expectation or through positional power, or is he able to persuade through personal power? Does she manage in an authoritative manner or is she able to be more developmental and democratic? Can he act independently, or does he prefer to achieve through a more conformist manner? Such questions and the information they elicit may be a more effective means of matching the person's self-understanding with the constraints on, and enhancers of, job performance, than are the well written descriptions of jobs.

It may be more important that managers making the choice of person try to be as aware as possible of proximate changes to corporate strategy. Those who advise on selection should therefore be very close to the corporate visionaries and strategists, needing to know what their view is of the change in the environment, what the demands on people are likely to be, what new challenges are likely to be faced. A dynamic understanding of the qualities needed for successful performance in a given position is vital; but it is unlikely to be given in the more traditional descriptions of jobs.

Having identified the changes to corporate strategy and the requisite personal qualities, HR may well be able to advise on, or make judgements about, individuals.

The people judgement process

The process requires people who are experienced and reliable judges of people, capable of understanding the limitation-trait theory, able to act as assessors rather than testers, able to understand that people are significantly more varied than a 'combination of traits' suggests.

Assessors as judges of others

Given the importance of some form of individual assessment to developing an understanding of people we need to briefly review the individual assessment process here.

The rapid expansion in the use of occupational tests has resulted in a considerable increase in the number of assessments and of people conducting them. Since each of these assessors is engaged in the process of judging another person, it is only appropriate that we ask how adept they are at this serious task.

There has been a considerable amount of research on the question of what makes a person an adept judge of others. Allport (1961) provided a list of the qualities likely to characterise a good judge of people.

Experience. An individual cannot judge others with whom he is not familiar

Similarity. It helps to have had experiences similar to those of the people being judged

Intelligence. The higher the assessor's intelligence, the better the judgement is likely to be

Cognitive complexity. Those who are more complex and subtle that the assessor will be more difficult to assess

Self-insight. Assessors who are prepared to self-assess are more likely to make sound judgements

Social skills and adjustment. Those who are free from neurosis and who are well adjusted, and have social and leadership skills, will be more likely to make effective judgements

Detachment. The effective judge is one who is sufficiently independent and objective

Aesthetic attitude. Those who are susceptible to artistic influence will judge others more effectively

Psychological mindedness. Those who have a tendency to understand themselves in a psychological frame of reference will have a major asset in judging others

Though these attributes may not be exhaustive or may not suffice to explain the totality of the effect of the assessor on the judgement process, they do draw attention to the need to understand the complexities of the judgement process. The assessor does not merely follow a set of predetermined administrative steps, which lead to a standardised assessment and a formula-based judgement, unless such is the objective. Assessment involves a complex process of behaviour analysis, which ultimately issues in judgement of a 'clinical' kind.

Murray (1938), provided a typology of assessors, who based their judgements he claimed, either on intraception or on extraception. Intraceptors tend to base judgements on subjective modes, on intuition and feelings; extraceptors tend towards objective data, norms and variable factors. The expansion of the testing market in recent years, may have produced a significant (and still growing) number of unsophisticated assessors who are reliant, predominantly, on the extraceptor process, which, because of its measurable criteria, is 'learned' more easily and quickly than intraception. The more 'sophisticated' approach to this form of assessment involves a combination of intraception and extraception, and this would require more experience on the part of assessors than could have been gained by recently trained practitioners.

The primacy that has been accorded to the 'test' may have

significantly reduced the role of intuition in assessment, result-
ing in a diminished appreciation, on the part of assessors, of
the complexities involved. It may well be that the limited value
given to intuition stems from the relatively short time allowed
for this topic on tester training courses. It may also be a result
of a failure by course examiners to consider the degree to
which trainee assessors are psychologically minded before they
are deemed effective. How many tester training courses
consider either before or during the course, the extent to which
the trainee assessor has 'the disposition to reflect upon the
meaning and motivation of behaviour, thoughts and feelings,
in oneself and others' (Faber, 1985)? Do they believe that if
assessors are insufficiently introspective or do not seek self
awareness or insight that they may not be capable of framing
adequate judgements about others?

If tester trainers consider only the ability of the trainee to
follow and apply the procedures required by the objective
approach, then they would be significantly limiting the development of assessors and diminishing the effectiveness of assessments made by them. Where their judgements are based
solely, or even primarily, on the outputs of the tests, in terms
of normative comparisons, it is unlikely that they will be
adequate assessments of the assessees. The assessor who
disregards the utility of non-test data, when making judgements, probably deserves the title 'tester' rather than
'assessor'. The tester will have administered a standardised
test, and scored and interpreted the data according to set
procedures but, will her or his judgements reflect a genuine
'understanding' of the assessee?

The assessor should be aware of *all* the clues provided by the
assessee during the testing session. The assessor should use the
assessment process as an opportunity to collect as much as
possible of the available data, which involves being 'open' to
all the information that the assessee provides.

It may well be that we should look to an assessment process
which has affinities with that which a therapist would undertake. Perhaps the assessor should seek to establish a diagnostic

alliance with the assessee. Perhaps it is only when the assessee perceives that the assessor is trying to understand his or her strengths, limitations and problems from his or her perspective, that assessees will open up sufficiently to provide the necessary personal information. This, however, will require that assessors are psychologically minded enough to recognise and encourage the greater breadth of personal information that is being sought.

The suggestions, therefore, are that there should be:

- some form of selection for psychological assessors which seeks to determine the degree to which they possess (or can develop) the attributes of the good judge stipulated by Allport
- an increased value placed on intuition, and more time devoted to 'psychological understanding' on tester training programmes
- continuing supervision of newly trained assessors, as there is for therapists, particularly if there is to be an emphasis on the model of diagnostic alliance.

Without changes such as these, standards in occupational psychology will, for many people, continue at the level of what 'the test' can evince. The judgements made of others will remain at the level of the extraceptor's limited data. The assessees may well be misunderstood, and individuals will make inadequate career and job choices. Therefore, from both a personal and an economic perspective, there is a clear need for a review of the competence of the assessor as a judge of others.

Means and methods for assessing others

Assessment has developed, particularly in the past decade, on the basic premise of 'physicalism'. The processes of scaling traits, which are conceived of as similar to physical properties, and norm referencing, are firmly in the physicalist tradition.

Trait theory has been the prime mover in psychometric development. 'The person' is typically conceived of as a combination of traits, held loosely together by the personal 'identity' of an individual. Not only is there a need to question the diminished understanding elicited by extraception, but the influence and value of physicalism as an appropriate model needs to be critically considered.

Physicalism gives rise to a number of significant problems when it is applied in the context of assessment. Assuming that every individual is constituted by some degree of every trait that can be identified, it would seem to follow that to describe a person fully requires that each trait be quantified. Unfortunately, it is impossible to measure such traits. Even if it were possible, it would be unnecessary, as most traits will have only limited value in an explanation of a given person. In addition, the individual, even if analysed in terms of thousands of traits, would not necessarily exhibit the numerous behaviours indicated by those traits. The effects of unconscious, or even conscious, restraints or enhancers would markedly alter behaviour, as also would the self-concepts. Thus, the physicalist description, even if it could be achieved in total, would still be an inadequate description of the person. Assessment from the perspective of traits is, therefore, flawed.

The physicalist model tends to lead the assessor in the direction of reductionism. If assessors follow the trait analysis, they may tend, to couch their interpretation in numeric form, perhaps through some desire to appear rigorously scientific. This reduction of the person to an equation or set of equations is an unjustified limitation of 'individual' status. The development of computer-based testing has extended the potential for reducing the person to an equation. The programmes seem to move assessment towards actuarial prediction.

The algorithms' mechanical rules dictate the computer's interpretation of tests. Relationships established between test scores and traits are fashioned into statements which are produced whenever an assessee produces a score which has been shown to be empirically related to these statements; and the statements are usually changed to incorporate the experience of the computer report's author. Because of difficulties in integrating the available data, the reports tend to become a combination of actual relationships, rules from other 'experts', and the author's own experience. The reports generated from computers are routinely amended. The assessor, who 'knows' the assessee, can make changes based on his or her judgement. HR professionals will amend reports which are based on their experience of a particular test or tests. Even with these personalised changes, the individual assessee continues to be defined as nothing more than a statistically significant trait pattern.

The computer may have made the process of test scoring more rapid. It may have quickened the process of interpretation. The ease of report production may have improved. It may, however, have made 'the individual' disappear even more under the welter of statistics, algorithms and traits that have replaced the person. The assessor, who begins to rely on the output of computer-generated reports, may well be in danger of losing the assessee and finding instead only a range of deviations from the norm.

Prehaps, like May (1958), we should seek to consider whether the fragmentation of the person is dysfunctional. He contends that the reality of 'the person' cannot be comprehended in a detached, abstract way – which is how a physicalistic approach would proceed. May considers that knowledge of the person can only be distilled from the total experience of the interaction between assessee and assessor.

Although a complete adherence to the existential perspective would appear to be somewhat difficult, in the normal client-and-assessor relationship in organisations, it would seem that there is a need to significantly modify the apparent risk of moving towards physicalistic reductionism. Perhaps, we should revive the humanistic perspective in its place. The drive towards a scientifically managed assessment environment, filled with assessments presented, scored, interpreted and reported by computer, should be evaluated in terms of the potential loss of the essential quality sought, 'the person'. Tallent (1969) would suggest that the physicalistic proposition is actually doing 'violence to the nature of man'.

HR professionals who work as assessors should perhaps be mindful that they, as assessors, could do violence not only to the assessee but also to themselves, if they scientifically manage 'people' out of the assessment equation.

The assessee as the assessor

Occupational testing has traditionally followed a procedure which comes to a conclusion when the assessor interprets the evidence and reports. Traditionally, therefore, the assessee has been regarded as the passive provider of information to the expert – the assessor – who evaluates the data and reports to the client. This view of the assessor as the expert also, perhaps, requires some examination.

HR professionals have had a tradition of regarding the finished product, 'the report', as somewhat hazardous if left in the hands of the assessee: it was considered to be potentially dangerous for the assessee to have sight of the content. Often the report, written for the client, would be accompanied by an explicit warning of the danger of showing it to the assessee. When the assessee was allowed to see the report, it was often on the basis of a selective review of the material. Sometimes assessees were provided with material from the report which had been 'censored' or defused to protect the innocent. The practice of sharing all the available data may, for some, have been considered a breach of ethics.

The argument seems to have been that the psychological terminology could so readily be misinterpreted by assessees that significant problems might occur. The assumption appears to be that if the HR professional – the expert – is not available on each occasion when the assessee has access to the report, there is a danger of the assessee misconstruing its content. Some would argue, further, that the assessee – who has, for example, a tendency to experience anxiety or depression – who reads a report which includes some negative comments may, if he or she is at that time subject to other stresses or depression, experience even more negative, anxious feelings. Thus there is a potential danger to the assessee's self-image.

Human Resources have a number of different methods of providing such reports. Some HR professionals still do not provide the assessee with feedback, except through the client – the person or organisation paying for the report. Many do not provide 'the full report' to the assessee, whilst a considerable number change the written report into a more 'acceptable' verbal feedback, for the 'benefit' of the assessee. Some produce two reports, one for the client and one for the assessee. Few share the unchanged written report in full. Even fewer produce the report jointly with the assessee.

Some reports, such as those produced by the computer-scored Strong Campbell Interest Inventory, are designed for the assessee to use, and it is common for these to be given to assessees, unedited, and they are then usually discussed with the assessor. Other computer-generated reports tend not to be, given into assessees' hands, probably because they are not particularly assessee-sensitive, and can appear stereotypical or edited.

It is worth considering, however, whether the report writing process should not be subject to review. If the psychologist is coming round, increasingly, to the view that the report is the joint property of the assessee and assessor, then perhaps the HR professional should also reflect on the need for change in this respect.

The assessee is almost certain to be able to give information about his or her thoughts, feelings and actions which would be a valuable addition or change to any report which had not taken account of the personal and 'subjective' dimension. Assessees are aware of what they would want others to know about them, and will be able to give examples of how particular traits have exhibited themselves. Information of this nature should be represented in an assessor's report. It would be useful if, for example, assessors' reports had space set aside for assessees to make their own comments, after having read the unedited versions – as is the case in the format of appraisal reports, which have become widespread over the past decade. It might also prove useful to the assessment process to provide assessees with a glossary of psychological terminology, and with interpretations of the psychological tests used. They could construct their own reports to supplement those of the assessors.

Assuming that assessors wish to develop a full 'understanding' of their assessees, it may well prove to be helpful if, having obtained the assessees' reports, assessors spend time exploring *their* interpretations and analyses and then for the two parties to jointly prepare an agreed version. Only when the data from assessments are shared *prior to* the preparation of reports, can we truly expect those reports to provide an understanding of the assessees' perceptions of their world.

If the object of assessment is to match the assessee with a work role, group or organisation, then there is an evident need to represent this assessee perspective. Assuming that there is agreement that assessees should contribute to the reports about themselves, then it would seem to follow that they should also be given opportunities to contribute to the verbal feedback to the client.

It is recognised that these practices of sharing data, joint report-writing and joint feedback, can be time consuming and logistically complex. However, as such assessments are usually undertaken in relation to important decisions, such as selection, promotion, management development and transfer, the time necessary for these joint procedures should not be seen as time wasted. Perhaps, employing organisations – which may well spend many weeks deliberating over a £1m capital decision – could be persuaded that a decision about a person who, in a lifetime's work, probably costs more than that sum in salary, and who may him or herself make *several* £m decisions, should be arrived at by means of a similarly circumspect process.

Assessees should be ascribed at least some of the assessors' role in respect of specifying or defining the competencies against which they are assessed. If they are already in-company, they may well have thoughts on the qualities needed for success. These should be shared. Assessees could also contribute to the assessment process by being given the time and opportunity to comment on the output of any psychological test or exercise they are asked to undertake. Perhaps, rather than being asked, later on, how they felt about a particular assessment process, they should be allowed to consider their feelings and thoughts *before* and *during* the exercise. If possible, assessees should be fed back the results of any assessment as part of the process, and asked to comment on how they feel about them. Do they fit with their self-concept? If not, how are they different? Can they give examples of past behaviour which illustrates any differences?

The process of assessment, in these ways, becomes one of dynamic interchange between assessor and assessee. Openness thus becomes more likely, and stereotyping less likely, and an improved assessment process will result (Ridgeway, 1992). An assessee should not be conceived of as a passive provider of data. Nor should the assessor be considered to be the objective and detached 'expert'. Assessment is a dynamic, interactive process, to which the assessee can contribute much.

HR professionals should seek to persuade their organisations that the additional time and expertise required to provide this kind of search for understanding are necessary on both economic and ethical grounds. Economically, it will provide better judgement and thus be more likely to result in improved performance. Ethically, because an inaccurate judgement may have profound and unwelcome consequences for an assessee, it is only just that an attempt is made to improve the balance and quality of interchange between assessee and assessor.

Assessment and 'the Person'

The use of psychometric instruments designed to measure personality has increased in line with the other assessment techniques already discussed. Decisions about selection, promotion, transfer and training are frequently made in light of the information derived from psychometric measurement.

One concern (and there are others), however, about the wide use of psychometric instruments is the assumption of testers that these instruments are measuring '*the* Person'. This assumption appears to lead 'psychometric technicians' to suppose that they have, through their instruments, been able to understand all aspects of the (unique) individual. Decisions are then taken on the basis of this understanding, which can be of 'life worth' determining significance: for example, a transfer to a company several thousand miles away, or a distinct change in career direction.

If Human Resource professionals believe that, through the use of their instrument, competently applied, they are enabled to capture '*the* Person', then there are considerable problems which may arise to confront them. One such problem concerns the efficacy of personality measurement, as such: to what extent might psychometric instruments be legitimately claimed capable of capturing '*the* Person'? The Johari Window provides us with a method of exploring this issue. A typical Johari Window is shown in Figure 12.1.

A would represent the elements of 'me' which you and I agree about. I know all about **A**; you know all about **A**, and we share that data. Most personality instruments would be able to capture and describe **A**.

B contains those elements which I know about me and which, at this time, I am not sharing with you. Depending on the circumstances, I may be prepared to share some, or all, of this self knowledge with you. Therefore **B** could become a set of responses which I might make in a personality inventory or questionnaire, given your ability to motivate me to disclose such data about myself, and my ability to articulate my sense of

Figure 12.1
The *Person, as seen through a Johari Window*

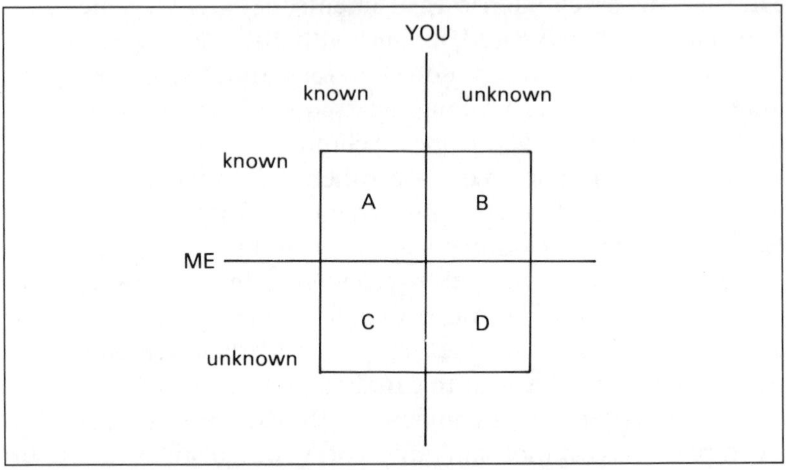

person. Under these circumstances, the information about me represented in **B** could be captured.

C contains what you know about me but are not disclosing to me. You may be able to articulate it in a counselling session focused on the result of a psychometric test; but it is unlikely to be articulated as the result of the test since, after all, it is *you*, not me, who has this knowledge. **C** therefore depends on the counselling skills of the assessor, and not on the psychometric measurement itself. (It is strange that most tester training programmes lack a significant counsellor training component or requirement.) It is possible that for some people **C** would be the largest cell in the matrix; yet, without the empathetic skills necessary to the successful development of my awareness of it, a large part of '*the* Person' would remain unknown to me, and decisions taken about '*the* Person' on the basis of my assessment will probably be of questionable value.

D provides a greater problem for those who rely on psychometric instruments to provide a description of '*the* Person'. **D** represents those elements of me of which I am ignorant, and of which you must be ignorant, too. Since all inventories rely on self-disclosure, they will be incapable of providing any evidence of **D**, and so would have to rely on the individual to provide any self-descriptions about whose disclosure they feel most comfortable with. Even so, these latter disclosures will not incorporate **D**, which remains unknown to both assessor and assessee.

For some individuals, '*the* Person' is most significantly enclosed in **D**. Such individuals are unaware of the motivating and inhibiting forces in their lives and these 'unconscious' forces may be, for them, the essense of '*the* Person'. Without knowledge of **D**, it is possible, even likely, that 'life worth' decisions could or would be taken, which may be significantly in error, and so could critically reduce 'life worth' for the individuals concerned. '*The* Person' can only be adequately described when **C** has been fully explored through counselling. This means that all assessors should have completed a counselling programme, if their objective is to provide a more complete understanding of individuals. **D** requires that methods other than the self-report inventory have to be considered.

Perhaps, therefore, a re-examination of the use of projective methods, for example, sentence completion or TAT (Thematic Apperception Tests) should be considered. It may be that the use of the interview should be explored. If **D**, the 'unconscious', needs to be explored in order to have access to '*the* Person' before we are in a position to how an individual might respond to, for example, promotion, transfer, or to selection decisions, we should consider whether the methods of the analyst, therapist and counsellor are not perhaps, after all, as potentially practicable and efficient as any recent personality measurement techniques.

In terms of our use of Johavi's Window, assessment appears to be relevant only for **A** and, potentially, for **B**, and for many individuals, these represent but a small part of '*the* Person': without **C** or **D**, they serve to describe only a limited extent of the individual's uniqueness.

We need to re-evaluate our methods, skills and our ethics, if we are to successfully enhance the 'life worth' of the individual and the worth of the individual to and for the organisation. Perhaps we ought to be moving the assessment process towards a combination of the critical evaluation of the individual's responses to a controlled situation and the interactive evaluation of responses within and outside the controlled stimuli. The application of the creative imagination to what the respondent may have been conceiving before, during and after the process may provide further insight into 'the Person'. We may be moving towards an agreement that feeling has a part in understanding the unconscious **D** level of 'the Person'. Perhaps, we can accept, as Hobson (1985) suggests for psychotherapy, that feeling is at the heart of assessment. A person meets a person, and provides a 'scientifically aware' judgement of 'the Person'.

Qualities that relate to successful management of change

There are several qualities that appear to relate to successful performance as a change manager. They include the recognition of the need to change, the ability to create a change vision and to persuade others to accept that vision, the capacity to manager others through the vision during change, and the personal qualities of independence, confidence, drive and resilience.

What might a composite of requisite and desired abilities, qualities and characteristics of the successful manager of change amount to? He or she would probably combine the following ingredients:

Cognitive capabilities

He or she would be

- open to possibilities, new explanations and ideas

- capable of recognising important issues and problems and isolating them from less pressing and peripheral matters
- quick to identify when current explanations may not be the most effective
- able and generally keen to assimilate a wide span of new information, and capable of efficiently extracting what is of most relevance to organisational requirements
- analytical in approach to problem solving and yet sufficiently imaginative to propose radically alternative solutions which are innovative and practicable.

Motivational profile

He or she would have

- a high level drive to take control of those resources which could be put to maximum use within his or her function
- a high level of personal achievement motivation
- the drive and authority to set his or her own objectives and to measure him or herself against self-imposed criteria
- a general sensitivity towards the needs and wishes of others without having a need to manage through, and influence by, affiliative means – creating harmony would not be at the top of this manager's list of priorities
- a capacity for expressing interpersonal warmth, while remaining relatively neutral in personal relationships
- a recognition of the importance of mutual interdependence, and respect between individuals.

Individual/personal qualities

He or she is likely to have

- a clear sense of autonomy
- a need for change and variety
- a capacity for flexibility

- a strong awareness of personal worth and morale
- a tolerance toward the opinions, values and ideas of others
- a high level of self confidence.

Such personal attributes need to be assessed pre-selection, development or transfer, against a matrix of clearly conceived, comprehensive and measureable indicators.

References

Allport, G.W. (1961) *Pattern and Growth in Personality*. New York: Holt, Reinhart and Winston

Murray, H.A. (1938) *Explorations in Personality*. London: Oxford Psychologist Press

Faber, B. (1985) 'The genesis, development and implications of psychological mindedness in psychotherapists'. *Psychotherapy, 27*, 170–177

May, R. (1985) 'Contributions to Existential Psychotherapy'. In R. May, E. Angel and H.F. Ellenberger *Existence* London: Basic Books

Tallent, N. (1969) 'Lightner Witmer's legacy'. *American Psychologist 24*, 473–475

Ridgeway, C.C. (1992) 'The Assessor: A valid and reliable judge of others'. *The Occupational Psychologist*

Strawbridge, S. (1992) 'Counselling Psychology and the Model of Science'. *Counselling Psychology Review 7*, 1 5–11

Polanyi, M. (1958) *Personal Knowledge*. London: Routledge & Kegan Paul

Hobson, R.F. (1985) *Forms of Feeling: The Heart of Psychotherapy*. London: Tavistock

13

▨ The Future – Developing Change Leadership Potential

Throughout this book, we have emphasised the need to pursue change strategies which empower people. Indeed, without this empowering component most change initiatives will fail. Our experience is that change leadership involves a continuous and increasing challenge, and we feel that the successful businesses of the future will be those which demonstrate the capacity for adapting and responding ahead of the competition. The identification and development of the distinctive change leadership competences associated with this capacity will be vitally important in creating a sound and lasting competitive advantage.

Increasingly, organisations need to review how they can facilitate an optimum response to change by harnessing the full co-operation and power of their staff. By helping individuals to recognise the need for change, and by empowering them to proactively manage their own careers, this power can be released. Recently, there has been considerable decentralisation and reduction of in-house training departments, and a corresponding rise of flatter, more open and more democratic organisations. This has presented new challenges for HR and line managers regarding how individuals may be helped to:

- become more aware of their attitudes and responses to change
- understand their strengths and weaknesses in relation to business requirements
- identify and direct their own career development via training and experience

Organisations of the future will be distinguished, also, by their ability to cope with global management, with the need for 24 hour business awareness, with growing market sophistication and complexity, with shorter product life, heightened competitive pressures and the broader span of control associated with the new, flatter organisations.

Over and above these requirements, both line and HR managers of the future will need to exhibit significant *change leadership potential*. They will need to be more intellectually able, in dealing with increasingly complex market information, with increasing degrees of ambiguity and uncertainty, and to have the capacity for providing visionary leadership while acting as role models for others.

The material presented in this chapter is based, in part, on our combined experience of assessing over one thousand senior executives during the past few years, and, also on empirical data collected from a sample of those managers and executives identified as being proactive in pushing ahead positive change in their organisations.

Firstly, we define what we mean by 'change leadership potential' and consider the specific personal qualities associated with change leadership potential. Then, we examine those aspects in the backgrounds of successful change leaders which seem to be related to their particular capacities for coping with change and which may be seen as influential in their development of the required competencies. Next, we focus on the issue of empowerment in order to clarify the term, and we examine with a case study on empowerment as part of a high profile change initiative. Finally, a summary draws together our proposals, and we pose a number of questions which may need to be raised.

Change leadership potential

Our emphasis on 'change leadership' indicates that the focus has moved along and that our concern is with proactive leadership rather than reactive management. It seems to us that the term 'change management' is used to refer more to an individual's response to change than to his or her potential, as a manager, to lead others through change. Until recently, change leadership seems to have been regarded as something only required when organisations were faced with the need to plan major change, which tends to imply a reactive stance in respect of change rather than a proactively recognition of the need for change and for initiating 'new' areas of change, previously unidentified.

We developed a questionnaire as part of a change management package. The package included a change leadership model, training in assessment techniques (together with a specially devised inventory), focused behavioural interviewing and OD consultancy support.

After discussions with a cross-section of managers involved in change, we piloted a form of the questionnaire, which included a range of items that might predict successful change leadership qualities. Approximately eighty senior managers involved in change were the respondents. They were divided in two groups: those who were seen as 'successful' change leaders and those who were not. Following a statistical analysis of the returned data, the Change Leadership Potential questionnaire was finalised and validated on about 100 volunteers.

Our analysis of the responses revealed that the successful change leaders tended to be significantly more:

- assertive
- sensitive, flexible and adaptable
- proactive and energetic
- mentally stable
- intellectually curious and open-minded
- able to handle a high level of ambiguity and to recognise complex patterns.

These qualities combine to provide a blend of intellectual ability, and influencing and counselling skills – all of which are required of the successful change leader.

Some of the personal history factors associated, in Chapter 9, with successful individual response to change were found, along with a number of new factors. The significant factors appear to be:

- having a secure family background
- being independent from an early age
- (probably) having a 'mobile family' when growing up
- being emotionally well adjusted and resilient
- having an effective support network (both formal and informal)
- being intelligent, innovative, forward-looking and open to new possibilities
- being flexible and people-centred
- being proactive and results-driven.

How this information is assessed, and integrated with other data in relation to a useful competency model, is important. Focused interviews, using behavioural evidence to support judgements, can overcome the major problems relating to subjectivity and bias in interviews. In order to go beyond the evidence of surface traits – i.e. what an individual 'knows' about him or herself and is prepared to share, we may, however, also need to probe using an in-depth psychological counselling interview.

Empowerment

How may an individual be truly empowered to manage personal change in respect of career development?

The term 'empowerment', as currently used, is clearly associated with moving away from the (benevolent) control and imbalanced power characteristic of hierarchical organisations of the past. Whereas, in the past, a manager might be sent on a course, with little say in the matter, nowadays this is relatively rare: the approach preferred would be for the individual concerned to be facilitated to understand his or her career objectives, to set the blocks in place, to identify training and development needs, and then proactively 'make it happen'. The term 'empowerment' is, however, often still spoken of in 'control' terms: e.g. 'how to empower your staff' or 'I empower you to . . .' and so on. This still implies an inherent power imbalance, i.e., the organisation or **I** (as its agent) **will empower you**. To do what? To do what *you*, as an individual, want? Or, to do what *we*, as an organisation (and I as its agent), want?

It is important to recognise that if an individual is to be *truly* empowered, this will necessitate letting go of control *altogether* and trusting the individual. Thus, as a manager or as a counsellor, I may *facilitate* your empowerment, but cannot be *responsible for* it. An anology might be in switching on an electric light. The illusion is that I empower the light. Actually, I only facilitate the system – by allowing the electricity to flow towards the element. I allow the light bulb to *empower itself*.

The implication for organisations is that, as well as having good communications – ensuring that everyone is in the picture and can see the need for change – they also need to provide the means for people to work out for themselves how they can best do what needs to be done, at an individual level, to meet the wider organisational goals. This may require counselling support to assess strengths and weaknesses; guidance may be required on the fit of these relative strengths with organisational requirements; and there could well be a need for further training and development, which is sometimes best sought for outside of the organisation altogether.

Clearly, successful change leaders need to be able to empower their staff by using a combination of visionary leadership and counselling skills.

A case study in empowerment – a Swiss merchant bank

A top-rated Swiss bank wanted to significantly increase the quality of its staff, including staff in the Training and Human

Resources department, while reducing corporate overheads. The HR director realised that, in order to respond more effectively to an increasingly competitive environment, training personnel needed to shift their overall resource profile from an already high starting point. This would necessarily require staff to proactively manage their own careers to help achieve the Bank's business aims.

The HR department began by inviting consultants to work with them, exploring aspects of the new culture and specifically the areas of competency which would help them to achieve the broader business aims. The culture was highly democratic and open, with a strong emphasis on persuasion, negotiation and achieving consensus. The business also recognised that, if they were to continue to compete effectively, they needed to capitalise on key technical and intellectual skills, as well as refined interpersonal skills.

As the business became leaner and more efficient, the centralised Training department was drastically cut back. The challenge was how the Bank could assess its staff, develop existing talent and optimise their human resource within the organisation, whilst also attracting new talent to raise its overall profile.

Having clarified their requirements through a series of competency exercises with key business units, the HR team decided to continue to use consultants in the next phase. It was felt that external consultants would be better placed than internal staff to bench-mark personnel against staff in competitor organisations in the market place, and that their assessment would be seen as fairer and more objective by staff. The consultancy team comprised chartered occupational psychologists who, together with the HR team, arrived at a process which could achieve the Bank's aims.

This may sound like a fairly standard, best practice, exercise with competency profiling following by standardised assessment procedures. There was, however, a distinctive element in the relationship between assessor and candidate: a clear contract was in place at the outset which stipulated that the major beneficiary in the exercise was to be the *individual member of staff*, rather than, as is usual, the client *organisation*. The message was that, in order for individuals to proactively manage their own careers (since the cut back in centralised training and development), they would need to better understand themselves. Their self-understanding was to be developed in relation to the business priorities, and individuals would work with the consultants to devise personal career development plans, to which the business would thereafter be committed.

The consultants worked in partnership with individuals in a 'developmental liaison' to help increase insight, and so allow them to empower themselves according to their own perceptions and priorities. The consultants were able to benchmark individuals in relation to best practice both outside and within the Bank. It was necessary, of course, to pass agreed information on candidates back to the HR department. This served to track the individual's development plan and also to contribute to a 'management audit' of existing intellectual ability, interpersonal skill and so on. In this way both individual and organisational effectiveness could be monitored. The consultants' role was, therefore, one of 'information broker', acting both for the organisation and for individual staff members.

The success of such an exercise depends largely on establishing trust, which comes from effective channels of communication, together with an adherence to the core purpose of empowering individuals rather than treating empowerment as just another 'flavour of the month'. It is also essential to have very clear contracts in such an exercise.

The Bank was able to significantly raise its competitive profile through a combination of restructuring, using most of its key talent, relocating some staff, and attracting high calibre new staff into the organisation.

Figure 13.1
Change leadership developmental process

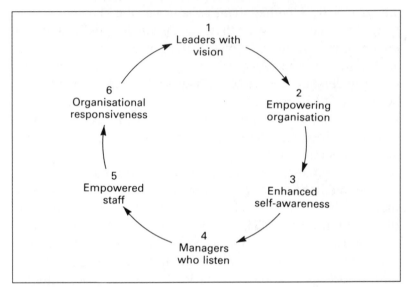

A change leadership model

Figure 13.1 shows the model for the overall developmental process. It presents a view of change as a continuous, pro-active, leadership initiative. As acceptance of a change-orientated culture builds, so too does empowerment and trust, and the process gathers momentum so that the organisation has an optimum response to international and local business pressures. Ultimately, the organisation will become a *change leader* rather than a merely effective respondent to imposed change.

Figure 13.2 shows the competency model for Change Leadership Potential. The hexagon represents the six basic competences, which themselves are contained within three broad domains. The triangle represents these three domains, which are:

Figure 13.2
Change Leadership Potential competency model

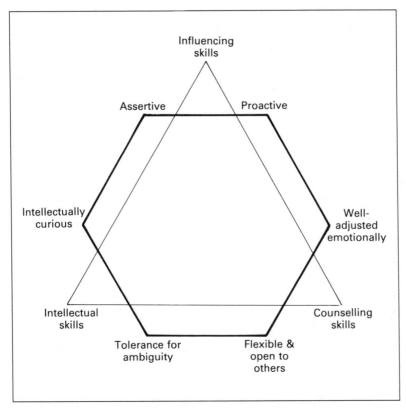

- *intellectual skills*: viz, intellectually curious and able to handle a high degree of ambiguity
- *influencing skills*: viz, assertive, and proactive and energetic
- *counselling and people skills*: viz, sensitive, flexible and adaptive around people, while having a high tolerance of pressure.

These competencies can be assessed by psychometric methods (including a specialised tool which we have developed). They may be used also in conjunction with other techniques, such as focused behavioural interviewing. Because the focus in the model is on personal qualities, rather than abilities, care needs to be taken not to underestimate their importance. To assess intellectual competence, it may well be necessary to use a battery of psychometric tests – measuring, for example, the individual's ability to process abstract and ambiguous information, their creativity under pressure – as well as assessing core management intellectual competences, such as numerical and verbal critical thinking.

Summary

Organisations of the future will be distinguished and ranked according to how well they can cope with

- global management
- 24 hour business awareness
- growing market sophistication and complexity
- shorter product life
- heightened competitive pressures
- the broader span of control associated with the new flatter organisations.

Both line and HR managers of the future will need to have a healthy and successful response to change. They will also need to exhibit significant *change leadership potential*. They will need to be more intellectually capable of dealing with increasingly complex market information and with an increasing degree of ambiguity and uncertainty. They will need to be able to provide visionary leadership, while acting as role models for others.

The key features of those individuals who are likely to be successful change leaders will include high levels of intellectual, influencing and counselling skills. Personal background factors may be important in identifying individuals who have the potential for developing these competencies. These factors may include demonstrating early independence of action from a secure family background, and having had a 'mobile family', or a similar experience. Having an effective support network (both formal and informal), as well as being emotionally well adjusted, with a high tolerance to pressure, are helpful in dealing with the likely stress arising from being at the cutting edge of change leadership.

Our examination of *how* these characteristics can be assessed and integrated into a total change leadership developmental process, hinged upon the notion of 'effective empowerment', which is a central tenet of developing staff to be in touch with how change issues affect them personally, and also to more readily lobby for their own training and development needs.

Some questions for HR managers to ask

1 Are we clear about the qualities associated with successful *response to change* as distinct from those additional qualities required for successful *change leadership*?
2 Can we identify those individuals who have a healthy response to change and those who may have a mal-adaptive change response pattern? (see Chapter 9)
3 Can we identify and assess the qualities associated with successful *change response*? (see Chapter 9)
4 Can we identify and assess the background factors and personal qualities associated with *change leadership potential*?
5 How can we support managers and executives in developing fully their *change leadership potential*? (see Chapter 11)
6 Are our communication channels open and clear?
7 What level of trust currently exists in our organisation?
8 How clearly do we understand the term 'empowerment'?
9 Can we counsel individuals on these issues in order to facilitate their empowerment?
10 Are we committed to an empowerment process and would

we maintain a high level of integrity throughout a change management initiative?

11 Do we tend to view change as an occasional reactive process or as a continuous and proactive *way of business life*?

14

▦ The Future – The HR Professional as a Strategic Partner

The world in which future organisations will operate is likely to be characterised by a wide range of problems, many of which will concern questions of structure, orientation, management style and culture. For example, organisations will need to decide on the extent to which they should be:

– integrated or differentiated
– formalised or informal
– entrepreneurial or risk averse
– tactical or visionary
– analytic or intuitive
– centralised or decentralised
– team-centred or individualistic
– flexible or focused.

The business environment is likely to be turbulent, complex and highly competitive. The foci of management attention are likely to include:

– innovation
– channelling entrepreneurial energy
– clarity of purpose
– integrating decentralised units
– creating effective teams comprised of self-sufficient individuals.

Motives and levels of motivation

If the HR advisor is to be enabled to perform successfully as line management's partner in the process of facilitating change, there will need to be a change in the focus of the HR role.

Traditionally, HR professionals have been 'company police-

Table 14.1
Company policeman profile

Motive	Motivation level		
	Low	*Medium*	*High*
Achievement to strive toward higher level achievements and continuous improvement	✓		
Affiliation Building and maintaining harmonious relationships	✓		
Power – Direct influence on others			✓
– Level of influence on organisation	✓		

men'. In this role, they have been seen as the guardians of the company's rules, procedures and practices, as these relate to human resources. The HR function acquired this 'policing' role largely because its personnel tended to have some expertise in employment law, salary systems, company procedures, etc. Their motives, and the related motivation levels exhibited, in performing this policing role are shown in Table 14.1.

When the HR professional becomes a 'developer', as many did, then he or she would need to exhibit different levels of motivation, in order to be successful. In the developer role, the HR professional's concerns as coach, counsellor and mentor to a range of staff, will require motivational levels in line with those shown in Table 14.2.

To become line management's challenging partner in the facilitation of optimum change strategies, the HR manager will need to exhibit a motivation profile like that shown in Table 14.3.

Table 14.2
Developer profile

| Motive | Motivation level | | |
	Low	Medium	High
Achievement		✓	
Affiliation			✓
Power			
– Direct		✓	
– Organisational		✓	

Table 14.3
Change partner profile

| Motive | Motivation level | | |
	Low	Medium	High
Achievement			✓
Affiliation	✓		
Power			
– Direct			✓
– Organisational			✓

To move from the role of corporate policeman to that of change partner, the HR professional will need to change the focus of his or her duties from the maintenance and application of quality policies, procedures and practices to the development of strategy. In this new role, the requirement is to help line management to conceptualize strengths and limitations and to visualise, innovatively, a strategic change programme. The HR professional will now be involved in implementing the programme by influencing and empowering line management to challenge the status quo and develop improved means of performing.

Strategic change partner competencies

The specific competencies required for this new role are shown in Table 14.4, along with the competencies required at the levels of company policeman and developer.

To perform successfully in this new role, HR directors and managers will need to assess themselves against the required competencies. The assessment should be self-applied, because one requirement of the new role is self-directed development. A schematic representation of the process by which the HR professional might develop these additional or enhanced competences is presented in Figure 14.1.

The self assessment component will probably involve the completion of a questionnaire designed to help the individual determine where he or she might have limited competence. The type of questions asked could include:

- Do you always seek novel solutions to any problem?
- Do you always try to visualise longer-term solutions when faced with a tactical problem?
- Do you always consider the impact of your words before you speak?
- Do you always remain sensitive to the effect of your non-verbal behaviour?
- Do you have a wide range of influencing styles?
- Do you always correctly identify the likely effect of any particular influencing style?
- Are you always resilient when under high levels of pressure?
- Are you always able to express an independent opinion?
- Are you always flexible in your thinking, attitudes and behaviour?

Skills training will probably focus on organisational development, the components of which will include: creating a learning culture in the organisation; developing entrepreneurial business capacities; encouraging staff to become self-

Table 14.4

Competencies required for particular HR roles

Competencies	Company policeman	Developer	Change partner
CORE COMPETENCIES	Required level	Required level	Required level
− job related	High	High	High
− commercial, organisational and financial awareness	Low	Medium	High
− inter-personal skills	Low	High	Medium
− communication skills	Medium	High	High
− customer focus	Low	High	High
− quality	High	High	High
− results	Medium	Medium	High
− self-management	Low	Medium	High
CHANGE AND INFLUENCE COMPETENCIES	Required level	Required level	Required level
− direct influencing	High	Medium	High
− organisation influencing	Low	Medium	High
− enterprise and risk taking	Low	Medium	High
− developing strategies for change	Low	Medium	High
− inspiring and motivating individuals and teams	Low	High	High

Figure 14.1
Development of change partner competencies

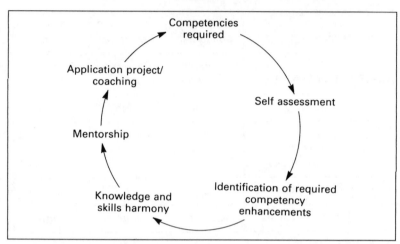

developmental; fostering openness and trust in interpersonal and team relationships; developing productive relationships between cross-functional teams; developing effective leadership and influencing styles; developing processes and procedures to enhance individual potential and organisational effectiveness.

The HR director/manager will need to develop a range of intervention skills, including: how to intervene, what skills to use to ensure the intervention is received positively, and how to remain open to change in a situation which might require change in the intervention's direction or emphasis. He or she will have to develop the capabilities to *gather data* on individuals, teams, organisations and climates, and from it to *diagnose* whatever problems exist. After diagnosis, he or she will need to be able to facilitate, together with line managers, the changes required. This, in turn, will mean that the HR manager needs to be persuasively authoritative in ensuring that his diagnosis is accepted by the top management and is integrated into the strategic plan. He or she must ensure that top mangers not only recognise the need to change, and also that it implements the required changes, in the optimum manner.

To achieve the highest level of effectiveness the HR director/ manager will need to recognise that senior management is not without occasional need of advice. He or she could encourage senior managers to avail themselves of HR support and counsel on matters ranging from diagnosing corporate requirements to meeting specific and personal counselling needs.

The HR director will need to understand the reasons why individual, or groups of, managers resist change and will act as counsel for line managers to ensure they develop appropriate skills and so increase their understanding of the organisation's environmental requirement to change.

The HR director will be a pace setter for the empowerment processes within his or her own department, and will frequently examine the department's values to gauge the extent to which they support the organisation's strategy. There will be a need for frequent self-examination to ensure the required level of personal visibility and influence: the capacity, skills and knowledge required to identify any opportunities to increase the effectiveness of both personal and departmental efforts, particularly in times of significant pressure.

As a strategic change partner, the HR manager will need to exhibit

- a sense of personal autonomy
- a high orientation to change
- an openness to new ideas
- a high level of personal psychological adjustment
- the capability to be an effective counsellor to a wide range of people at managerial levels and in socially and culturally diverse contexts
- a high level of self confidence
- personal flexibility in attitudes and style.

As a departmental director/manager, he or she will be able to exhibit, in dealings with other directors/managers:

– a wide range of leadership styles
– a wide range of influence styles
– a high level of respect for, and interest in, others' views and
  opinions
– a capacity for developing personal relationships.

Some problems and issues for HR directors/managers

Acting as a strategic partner can create significant problems for
the director/manager. Some of the HR staff will not have the
competency necessary to the change facilitator role: they will
not be able to conceive at the level required; they will not be
intellectually capable of analysing or innovating at the level
required. The HR director/manager has to decide, therefore,
how to career counsel such staff: what action should be taken
regarding their transfer, development or outplacement? Whilst
achieving this objective, he or she has to ensure that other
departmental staff remain satisfied and motivated.

Among the numerous issues which HR managers are likely
to have to address at some stage are:

- meeting training needs of individuals: ensuring that those
  departmental staff who have development needs are coached
  and counselled to achieve the required competencies
- procedural maintenance: ensuring that the requirements of
  HR's 'hygiene' role – as custodian of corporate policies and
  practices – are effectively and efficiently carried out
- maintaining professional confidentiality and integrity: given
  that they are likely to become counsel to the Managing
  Director, they will have to ensure that their feelings for
  senior managers and directors do not negatively influence
  their advice on transfers, promotions and outplacement of
  senior staff.
- maintaining the focus on the organisation's vision.

HR directors/managers need to ensure that they, their own

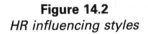

Figure 14.2
HR influencing styles

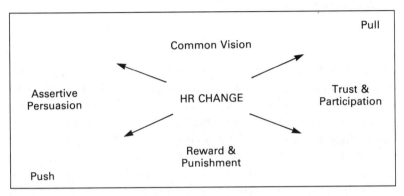

staff, and the total workforce recognise: the need to change; the future vision; the steps to achieve the vision; and the benefits in store for the organisation as a whole.

HR influencing styles

HR managers will need to exhibit in their own team and in the organisation a range of influence styles from push to pull (see Figure 14.2). They will generally need to ensure that the personnel managerial and organisational philosophy supports the corporate strategy.

They will need to use a range of influencing approaches to ensure that managers and their teams move

- from a defensive to a responsive attitude to change
- from an internally conceived to an externally determined pressure for change
- from a 'tell and see' approach to management to an 'ask and listen' style
- from an individual perspective on change to an organisational viewpoint
- from a short term to a long term strategic perspective.

■ Empowering Change – A Postscript

In our Introduction, we stated our aim to illustrate practical, business-relevant, approaches to successful change. We also indicated that change in business organisations involving people was a complex topic. Our book was designed to present the change agenda faced by management. We hope that you will be able to take away some valuable insights. The complexity of our topic means that no simple message can be drawn out. However, as a postscript, we would wish to re-emphasise the following key messages:

Successful change management

In terms of our overview of successful change covered in Chapter 1 to 3, the key insights are:

1. A specific and succinct statement of the business rationale in change is essential
2. Successful change requires a market focus and statement of the competitive advantage sought
3. Leadership behaviour in change is crucial
4. In planning change a philosophy of empowerment is required, so that change does not become a threat and a constraint
5. Change needs to be seen as on-going evolution based on real learning and understanding
6. Culture and people matter in change, because new behaviour is an essential requirement
7. The changing world requires a new philosophy of management

8. All of the stakeholders in change, both internally and externally, need considering
9. Any strategy for substantial change requires a shared vision based on a coherent set of values and beliefs.
10. The concepts of ownership and commitment will make the difference.

Lessons from our case materials

The case material presented, we believe, describes the real world of change. The change agenda presented covers many of the challenges faced by businesses in terms of:

- rationalisation and restructuring
- internationalisation
- market leadership
- mergers and acquisitions
- the casualties of change

The lessons drawn are:

(a) *In restructuring and rationalisation*

- it is important to evaluate the cost/benefit in change from both the economic and people standpoint
- a clear choice is needed between an evolutionary or revolutionary approach
- a thorough planning phase is essential to address the broader fundamental issues; to do this on the run will not work
- regular reviews and feedback can provide the opportunity to stop and think and also to move from revolution to evolution
- rebuilding of trust is an essential consequence of rationalisation
- new concepts of the career contract will be needed

- energy should be focused on the 'stayers' as well as the 'leavers'.

(b) *On business internationalisation*

- clear definitions are needed on the roles required and competencies needed for international success
- selection is crucial, since not all managers can succeed
- developing people for international roles will require distinctive and systematic career planning
- expatriate stress can exist and needs managing
- a new business start-up overseas will involve a back-to-basics approach
- national culture matters and the introduction of Western management philosophies needs careful and empathetic introduction.

(c) *On market leadership*

- a new business focus will require a review of the people and organisational needs
- competency assessment and development provides a vehicle for measuring for high performance and best practice
- in seeking leadership and innovation a new management style and approach will be needed
- an external focus and benchmarking will be required
- quality people will require different management roles, career opportunities, reward and recognition.

(d) *On mergers and acquisitions*

- people and cultural fit are essential for success
- the pre-decision making process will require such data on people systems
- 'due diligence' can provide the opportunity to look at senior managers and their people systems and practices
- thorough integration will be needed, born out of an open

consideration of the strengths of both parties; subordination of one will exact a price in terms of success
- a new identity for both will be required, against a shared vision and a common set of values and beliefs.

(e) *On the casualties of change*

- insights about the individual's personal make-up make the difference in redeployment
- redundancy can substantially affect individuals' self-esteem and motivation, which needs careful and intelligent rebuilding
- the ability to adapt to change will be essential for the manager of the future.

Implications for the future

We have presented a broad array of insights here.

(a) *For the young manager*

- a whole new concept of career management is needed
- managers should be encouraged early on to take responsibility for their own futures
- early experience with effective coaches can develop the right attitudes.

(b) *For the HR function*

- the challenge is to determine the role and influence sought and acceptable
- the concept of the strategic change partner will require new competencies, a broader range of concepts and experience, different selection and development processes
- the transition from custodian of the HR system to internal

HR consultant will be both demanding and inevitably needed.

(c) *In assessing people who will succeed in a changing world*

- a clear understanding of the new roles and competencies sought will be required
- assessing people will require not only measuring, through psychometrics, but also a concern for the whole person and their right to determine their own future
- judges need to question their own rights in influencing others' futures.

(d) *For the successful manager of the future*

- change leadership competencies will be essential
- our research shows the distinctive qualities needed
- a critical mass of change ability will need developing as organisations continuously strive to adapt and respond ahead of the competition.

Our core message throughout the book has been the need to strive for an empowering philosophy and approach. The above insights demand a thorough consideration of the impact of change on the business leader, the HR function, the individual manager and staff. Future business success will require an empowering philosophy. For the line manager and the HR professional, the gauntlet has been thrown down. We hope that our book will encourage you to pick it up.

Our last thought is that, in change, *people make the difference.*

About the Contributors

Dr Lea Brindle is a Chartered Occupational Psychologist with several years' consultancy experience. He is Principal of Psychological Solutions Consultancy and an associate of the ODL Partnership. He has also worked as a consultant with Coopers & Lybrand and with a leading firm of occupational psychologists. He currently specialises in career management research and practice and has counselled over three thousand senior managers and professionals in recent years.

Trevor Johnson is HR Director of Reckitt & Colman Products Ltd, although his previous career was in marketing – a background which has enabled him to implement business-relevant HR strategies.

David Patterson is General Manager for Corporate Affairs at Zurich Insurance, with special responsibility for internal and external communications. He has had 25 years' HR and general management experience in blue-chip companies both in the UK and in Europe.

John Refaussé is Director of HR Development in the Hiram Walker Group, the Wines and Spirits subsidiary of Allied-Lyons plc. His current interest is in assessing the impact of the internationalisation of the business on the roles and competencies needed for market leadership.

Len Sheen is HR Director, Europe and Far East, for the Hiram Walker Group, the Wines and Spirits subsidiary of Allied-Lyons plc. He has over 20 years' experience in HR management, having worked for Guinness plc, Max Factor Inc. and Combustion Engineering Inc., specialising in the international aspects of organisational development.

Ashley Wood is Manager, Personnel Development at Meyer International plc, an international distributor of building materials and timber. His career spans the armed forces, line management and, over the last 10 years, human resource development; he has worked in Europe, the United States and Japan.

Index

16PF (psychological test) 132–3

Acquisitions and mergers 43,
    110–28, 204
    see also Mergers
Allied-Lyons (case study) 84–97
Al-Prut (case study) 84–97
Appraisal, competency-based 106
Assessment
    humanistic approach to 170-71
    input from assessee 171–4
    methods 168–74
    and *'the* Person' 175–8
    physicalist/reductionist model of
        168–71
    qualities needed for 165–74, 206

Behavioural Events Interviews 102
Benefits, for international managers
    83–4
Brakel, Aat (*People and
    Organizations Interacting*)
    19–20

Capacity to change, individual
    163–80
Casualties of change 6–7, 129–41,
    205
    support for 138–9
Change
    attitudes to 10–16
    casualties of 6–7, 129–41, 205
    history of 11–21
    individual capacity for 163–80
    language of 4–5, 33–4
    resistance to 1–2
    revolutionary and evolutionary
        58–9, 61, 65
    responses to 129–41; *see also*
        Responses to change
    stakeholders in 30–32, 33
Change agendas 5–6, 46–9, 69
Change agents 9–10

Change leaders, managers' role as
    5, 8–9
Change leadership potential 136–7,
    140, 181–92
    competency model 188–190
    defined 182–4
Change management, critical
    success factors for 7–8, 20–21,
    28, 30, 33, 178–80, 203
Change partnerships, between line
    and HR 2–4
Change strategies 26–30, 33
Communications 62–3, 120–21, 125
Compensation, for international
    managers 83–4
Competency appraisal processes
    106
Competency development centres
    102–5
Competency development
    programmes 106–7
Competency selection systems
    105–6
Consultancy role of HR 18, 48
Critical success factors, in change
    management 7–8, 20–21, 28,
    30, 33, 178–80, 203
Cycles of frustration 2

Delayering 39–40
Development, of international
    managers 82–4
Development centres 102–5
Development programmes,
    competency-based 106–7
Directors, HR 198–201
Diversity, management of 19
Downsizing 39–40

Eastern Europe, business start-up
    in (case study) 84–97
Empowering HR teams 49

Empowerment
    and change 1–3, 10, 18, 145–9,
       184–7
    defined 143–4
    values 22–4
Enabling strategy for change (Shell)
    61–5
Evolutionary versus revolutionary
    change 58–9, 61, 65
Expatriate stress 78–9

Furnham, Adrian 113–14

Graduate recruitment 105–6
Gunter, Barry 113–14

'Hard'/'soft' approaches to change
    management 17–20
Hiram Walker (Allied-Lyons case
    study) 84–97
HR directors, issues for 198–201
HR function
    and assessment 163–4
    as challenging partners in change
       34–7, 78, 81, 82, 83–4
    as change consultants 18, 48
    as change facilitators 35–7
    changing role of 37–45, 193–5
    competencies needed by 197–201
    empowering role of 37–45, 49
    influencing styles 201
    and internationalisation 76–8
    leadership values 22–4, 25
    and marketing function 98–9
    as strategic partners in change
       2–4, 9–10, 34, 35–7, 44, 100,
       193–201, 205–6
    traditional and empowering roles
       of 37–45
    value added by 44–5
HR managers, issues for 198–201

Individual responses to change
    129–41, 163–80
Influence mapping 45–8
Influencing styles, for HR 201
International managers 80–84

Internationalisation 40, 76–97, 204
    HR role 76–8

Joint ventures, international (case
    study) 84–97
Judging people, qualities needed
    for 165–74

Leadership styles and values, in
    change 22–34, 59–61, 65–6
Leeds Permanent Building Society
    (case study) 11–12

Managers, as change leaders 5, 8–9
Managers, HR 198–201
Managers, new, introducing into
    organisations 142–9
Market leadership, achieving 42,
    98–109, 204
Marketing competency study 101–2
Marketing function 98–9
Mergers and acquisitions 43,
    110–28, 204
    assessment of senior management
       113–15
    and communications 120–21, 125
    and culture 117–18
    failures 110
    incompatible management styles
       111–12
    and IR 120
    matching people to jobs 117
    and personnel procedures 118–19
    post-merger role of HR 121–3
    pre-merger research 110–11
    pre-merger role of HR 113–15
    terms and conditions of
       employment 126
Meyer International 142
Municipal Mutual Insurance (case
    study) 124–8

National and Provincial Building
    Society (case study) 111–12
New (young) managers 142–9

OPQ (psychological test) 132–3

Person, *the*, and assessment
    methods 175–8
Personality
    dimensions 133–4
    and job success 132
    and responses to change 129–41
Personnel, changing role of 45
Psychometric testing 135–6
Physicalist/reductionist model of
    assessment 169–71

Rationalisation, *see* restructuring
Rebuilding trust, after major
    change initiatives 150–62
Reckitt and Colman Products (case
    study) 99–109
Reductionism, in assessment 169–71
Redundancy 6–7
Responses to change, individual
    assessment of change
        competencies 136–7
    background factors 130–31
    personality factors 131–6
    psychometric tests 135–6
    successful 136–7, 183–4
Restructuring
    costs and benefits of 52
    lessons for HR 71–5
    management of 38–9, 50–74,
        203–4
Revolutionary versus evolutionary
    change 58–9, 61, 65
Royal Dutch Shell Group (case
    study) 53

Selection, of international managers
    80–82

Selection systems, competency-
    based 105–6
Self-empowerment 145
Shell International (case study) 19,
    53–71
'Soft' approaches to change
    management 17–20
Stakeholders in change 30–32
Strategic change partnership
    competencies, for HR 196–200,
    205–6
Structural change, at Shell (case
    study) 55–8
Succession management 142–3
'Survivor' syndrome, after mergers
    126
Swiss merchant bank (case study)
    185–7

Thriving on change 129–41
Trust
    assessing levels of 154–5
    breakdown of 153–4
    defined 151–3
    and management competencies/
        behaviours 157–8
    measuring damage to 156
    rebuilding/repairing 154–62

values, leadership 22–34

young people, as managers 142–9,
    205

Zurich Insurance (case study) 124–8

Other titles in the Developing Strategies series

Managing the Mosaic
Diversity in action

*Rajvinder Kandola
and Johanna Fullerton*

**Special Commendation winner at the
1995 Management Consultancies Association Book Awards.**

Today, all organisations have to confront the challenge of diverse workforces. Yet many equal opportunity initiatives, in particular target-setting and positive action, which focus on specific groups such as women or ethnic minorities, are fundamentally flawed. To be effective, diversity strategies must tap into the talents of all staff, not just those from selected groups.

In this provocative but highly practical book, Rajvinder Kandola and Johanna Fullerton – chartered occupational psychologists at the Pearn Kandola practice in Oxford – set out to separate myth from reality. Drawing on a wide-ranging literature search, extensive experience of working within companies, and a survey of almost 300 organisations they give clear evidence that group-based equal opportunity policies are divisive and seldom successful.

Effective diversity strategies, pioneered by companies such as International Distillers and Vintners, are summed up in a detailed new model and linked to the ideal of the 'learning organisation', whose essential elements are flexibility, an empowering culture, universal benefits and business-related training for whoever needs it. Demographic changes, legislation, and increasingly globalised markets mean that diversity is now of central concern for all employers. This book provides definitive solutions to their problems.

> '[*Managing the Mosaic*] makes a compelling case for the better management of the resources of the business: people with their wide variety of attributes, concerns, values and needs.'
> *The judges' panel, 1995 MCA Book Awards*

1994   200 pages   Royal paperback   ISBN 0 85292 556 5   **£17.95**

Leadership for Strategic Change

Christopher Ridgeway
and Brian Wallace

Effective strategic change leadership means seeing beyond day-to-day issues towards forging a new vision for the business. It means using influence to get others on board or facilitating them to achieve results. It also means choosing the right style – flexible, participative or more controlling – to adopt in specific circumstances.

This superb book enables potential change leaders to think through the issues, assess their core skills, put them into context and proceed to action. Stimulating questionnaires test for different kinds of leadership ability. Vivid case-studies spell out lessons in organisations that have undergone major change, and frank extended interviews with key players in change initiatives offer invaluable insights.

1996   240 pages   Royal paperback   ISBN 0 85292 613 8   **£18.95**

Changing Culture
New organisational approaches

*Allan Williams, Paul Dobson
and Mike Walters*

This invaluable book draws on the experiences of major organisations to reveal how culture change can help drive through significant improvements in performance, efficiency, and profitability. Strategic thinking is vital, but the core personal skills – appraisal, communication, remuneration and training – also play a key role. The book explains just why culture remains crucial, and includes stimulating, up-to-date case-studies from the Royal Mail, McVitie's, Exxon UK, and James Cropper plc.

'One of the most useful recent works on corporate culture
. . . a good starting-point for any manager.'
Long-Range Planning

1993   Second edition   328 pages   Royal paperback
ISBN 0 85292 533 6   **£18.95**

Ethical Leadership

*Stephen Connock
and Ted Johns*

Today's managers are constantly faced with acute ethical dilemmas; many may feel under pressure to sacrifice personal beliefs to corporate gain. Yet most books on business ethics are obscure and overtheoretical. This bold new text adopts a considered but completely practical approach that has nothing to do with saintliness and everything to do with organisational effectiveness and management action. Topics covered in depth, with stimulating company examples, include:

- balancing the needs and perspectives of different stake-holders
- codes of business conduct and common ethical issues about gifts, hospitality, confidentiality and conflicts of interest
- establishing the values to promote the right behaviour
- implementing core principles
- the roles of training and HR.

1995   240 pages   Royal paperback   ISBN 0 85292 561 1   **£18.95**